NIGHTFARING

NIGHTFARING

IN SEARCH OF THE
DISAPPEARING DARKNESS

MEGAN EAVES-EGENES

**SIMON &
SCHUSTER**

London · New York · Amsterdam/Antwerp · Sydney/Melbourne · Toronto · New Delhi

First published in Great Britain by Simon & Schuster UK Ltd, 2026

1 3 5 7 9 10 8 6 4 2

Simon & Schuster UK Ltd, 1st Floor
222 Gray's Inn Road, London WC1X 8HB

Simon & Schuster Australia, Sydney
Simon & Schuster India, New Delhi

www.simonandschuster.co.uk
www.simonandschuster.com.au
www.simonandschuster.co.in

The authorised representative in the EEA is Simon & Schuster Netherlands BV,
Herculesplein 96, 3584 AA Utrecht, Netherlands. info@simonandschuster.nl

A CIP catalogue record for this book is available from the British Library

Hardback ISBN: 978-1-3985-3294-6
eBook ISBN: 978-1-3985-3296-0

Typeset in Bembo by M Rules
Printed and Bound in the UK using 100% Renewable Electricity
at CPI Group (UK) Ltd

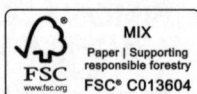

MIX
Paper | Supporting
responsible forestry
FSC
www.fsc.org   FSC® C013604

For Dad, who gave me the stars and wanderlust.
And for Dan, who told me to travel and write.

Contents

GOING INTO THE DARK

It's cold. I'm not sure how cold because I haven't checked my phone, but the temperature has been dropping since the sun set hours ago. A layer of frost on the garden table sparkles from light spilling out of a neighbour's upstairs window.

I park myself on one of the frosting-over chairs facing south. South is the best direction to look for any attempt at stargazing in London. This is especially true if you are south of the River Thames because you are facing away from the centre of the city, the main source of light at night. In winter at this latitude, to the south, there is a reasonable view of the seasonal highlights in the sky: Orion, Sirius, Capella, the twin stars Castor and Pollux in the constellation Gemini, and my favourite, a little cluster of stars called the Pleiades.

I am a winter person. I grew up at a high elevation in the southwestern United States, and the arid winds are in my blood because sitting outside in cold weather and looking at the winter sky is my idea of perfection.

It might seem counterintuitive to go stargazing in a huge city. If you've ever looked up into the night sky in a place like London, New York or Hong Kong, you know that too much artificial light has bleached the sky, making it impossible to see the stars. This washed-out sky – an insipid yellow from wasted light particles scattering up into the air – is a phenomenon called skyglow. It happens because lights are kept on when they aren't necessary, fixtures aren't pointed downwards, bulbs are left bare or unshielded, and curtains and blinds aren't closed. On a clear London evening, you might be able to see only ten stars of the roughly 5,000 that would be visible in a truly dark area.

Tonight, I pull a blanket around my shoulders and breathe in the sharp air, wishing away the neighbours' light even though I know better – they keep it on all night.

I can trace the journey that follows in this book to a night just like this one, almost a decade ago, when I arrived home from a late-running work event and immediately sought solace under the stars in the garden. I poured a glass of Malbec and squinted through the skyglow.

That version of me didn't realise that she was facing into a period of darkness that would change the entire trajectory of her life. Within a year, my beloved stepfather would pass away and my marriage would crumble. Within two, I'd be made redundant from my dream job, and within three, the whole world would be plunged into the dark stillness of a global pandemic. That night, I was just hoping to see the same stars I remembered from my childhood in the northern New Mexico desert.

In the years that followed those events, I used garden stargazing as therapy. I mourned, wept, reflected and meditated under the night sky. A lifetime of pent-up trauma was unleashed under the unbothered stars. I confronted darkness as both a natural habitat and a metaphorical and spiritual condition. The more time I spent in darkness, the more it seemed to heal me, and the more I yearned for its quiet embrace.

Eventually, I wasn't so sad any more, and the stars were still there, rising after the sunset and setting with the seasons. Summer turned to autumn, winter frost, then spring daffodils. Another year with more challenges, joy, laughter and faces new and familiar. Some more things were lost, and some were gained. Still, the stars kept me company. It gave me solace to know they had seen it all before – every anguish, every word written, every mistake made – and they would be there for an eternity after me.

But knowing that the full, starry grandeur was blocked from my view also made me long to escape the skyglow. I began studying astronomy and travelling to dark locations to see the stars. I learned about light bulbs, light-emitting diodes and shields, and got involved with advocacy against light pollution. From this longing, I set out to truly understand the dark. To try to comprehend why we are quickly destroying it, what drives our fear of the darkness, how humans have interacted with the night from ancient times and what the future may hold. My search ended up taking me across the world, from my homeland in New Mexico to Mount Everest, from the North York Moors to the Argentinian jungle, and many dark patches in between.

Looking at the stars is one of the activities in human existence that elicits true wonder. That feeling of excitement, of the unknown; a sense of the ancient and everything that came before us and that will follow us. The stars have inspired art, music, poetry and storytelling through every human age; they have guided our feet, our ships and our satellites, and given us the ultimate gift of creative inspiration.

The only time I feel a real sense of perspective is when I'm looking up at the night sky, because I'm reminded of how tiny I am and how insignificant my problems are. At the same time, it makes me feel like I, on this speck of rock, am still part of something – a being inextricably linked with the entire unfathomable universe.

This deep yearning to be overwhelmed by the star map overhead never goes; it is an engine constantly running in the background of my emotional life. And so, any time a cloudless night presents itself, I am outdoors, looking up, straining through skyglow to see a few twinkles of light from a distant sun to feel the cosmic grandeur that connects us all.

1

HOME

New Mexico & London

I'm not sure how old I was the first time I really looked up at the night sky. It is a hazy memory of a dry summer night, the pine scent of piñon trees and dust in my nose, and the sky like a bowl of ink overhead. I was probably about five.

In 1986, we lived in a little adobe house on a large plot of pastureland 20 miles south of Santa Fe, New Mexico, in the southwest US. In the 1950s, my grandfather had bought up a huge tract of land next to hills that were once among the most prolific turquoise-producing areas in North America. Before that, it had been the land of the Indigenous Ya'atze people, who left the area after taking part in the Pueblo Revolt of 1680 – an uprising against Spanish colonisers. Even now it is a place most people would struggle to point to on a map. My parents had been real bluegrass hippies and were now emerging into the 'capitalist wonderland' of Ronald Reagan's 1980s, raising a young family but still eschewing tradition by living partially off the grid.

In the middle of nowhere is what I told my friends at school in town when they asked where I lived. I didn't know how else to describe where my house was – it wasn't part of the city and it wasn't on a street, and that made me feel strange and out of place. At home, though, everything felt right. After a long day at school, my parents would pick us up and zoom out of town, then down our mile-long dirt driveway. It was just off Highway 14 and then off State Road 285 and up onto a small bluff, below which a sandy arroyo – the New Mexico version of a dry riverbed – ran with flash floods during August monsoons. The arroyo was dusty and made a good place to play *Zorro* or *The Lone Ranger* or epic and unbeatable rounds of hide and seek when our big-city cousins from Albuquerque came to visit.

My dad, an astronomy buff, had a white telescope that took pride of place in the living room. I asked him recently and he told me it was a six-inch, Meade reflector telescope, of average size, but to me back then it seemed massive. It stood leaning diagonally on a big metal mount, as tall as he was – which to kid-me felt like the Empire State Building. On nights when there were very particular things to see, he would haul it out to the dirt driveway in front of the house.

The skies above northern New Mexico in 1986 had a lot of things to see. Actually, all of the things to see. So it took a special event, like an eclipse, a planet passing very close to the Moon, or Halley's Comet – which we spent many evenings looking for that year – to wheel the big telescope out from its throne. My dad would set it up, spending what felt like hours making tiny adjustments to little protruding lenses, spinning small black knobs and gently swaying the white cylinder back and forth until it rested in just the right position.

This bit, for a little girl, was mostly boring, but being outside at night was exciting, and being with Dad was a thrill. We learned to read a star chart, carefully sliding its lower layer around to match the arrows with the month and day, and then squinting to compare this handheld map of stars to the real sky above.

Dad knew a lot about the stars and would recite their names and the constellations as if they should mean something to me at such a young age. *There's Perseus. That's Auriga next to it. There's Orion, see his belt with the three bright stars? That little cluster, that's the Pleiades – the Seven Sisters.* My sister Juels, and I liked the Pleiades the most because it looked like a tornado made of stars that were sisters.

Growing up on ranch land in 1980s New Mexico turned me into a pretty feral child. Like most kids of my generation, I was set loose outside to play and entertain myself until dinner time, and my parents were both busy running independent businesses – my dad was a leather craftsman who made belts, bags and saddles, and my mother ran a successful pet-related business.

During the day, I was always outside. I learned my environment like it was my own skin. I had no idea how to ride a subway train, wasn't so good with people and had trouble making friends at school, but in the desert I was perfectly at home. I knew how to avoid rattlesnake bites, which plants were poisonous to our horses, and what to do in the event of a flash flood in the arroyo. I could tell you the locations of the only natural springs within 5 miles of the house, and how to get water from a prickly pear cactus if I ever had to.

There were also desert storms to be reckoned with. Though it rarely rained, during the monsoon season in July and August, the afternoon and evening storms came fast and fierce. The arroyo below the house was bone dry until it wasn't, and it didn't have to be raining in your location for there to be a flash flood – they started in the mountains. Every year, there was a headline about an unsuspecting person washed away in an Albuquerque gully. *If you ever see water, even a tiny bit of water, in this arroyo, run straight out of here as fast as you can.* The instructions were drilled into me, as was a deep and abiding respect for and fear of the nature around me. You had to know how to live as part of the land because you sure as hell couldn't control it.

We didn't have street lights or any exterior illumination at our house, apart from a single front door light that was switched off as soon as we got in, so it didn't attract insects. We weren't allowed to go outside at night without an adult, and I knew well why. If the desert was wild during the day, it was lethal at night, when coyotes, mountain lions and scorpions were out.

This made nights out looking at the stars with Dad all the more meaningful. It was one of the few times we were allowed to be outside, and the memories are of soft darkness and a sky full of stars wrapped like a blanket all around us. This instilled in me the idea that the night could be both peaceful and dangerous, and it taught me how to appreciate the beauty of nature while also respecting its complete power over me.

The New Mexico sky now looks vastly different from the way it did in the 1980s. South of Santa Fe, it remains mostly dark, but even in such a rural and unspoilt place – still the middle of nowhere – the creeping glow of light pollution from Albuquerque inches over the tops of the Sandia Mountains, spreading north like yellow oil, threatening to erase the Big Dipper and the North Star.

I moved around a lot in my twenties: spent time teaching English in China, where the sky was polluted both day and night; did a master's degree in Dublin, Ireland, and spent a romantic but difficult year as a broke freelance writer in Prague. During this period, far from home, I didn't think about the night sky at all. It had completely disappeared from my physical and emotional reality.

But then I landed in London, and something about life in a big city stirred up a yearning for the stars. But the more I tried to stargaze from my back garden in Lewisham, the more aware I became that the night sky was a bleached void, and the more my craving for the stars grew.

I started planning trips to see the night sky. First to deepest North Wales, then the Scottish Highlands. A camping trip to a 'Dark Sky Sanctuary' back in New Mexico introduced me to the work of DarkSky International, the organisation responsible for certifying such darkness preserves around the world.

At work, at the travel publisher Lonely Planet, I wouldn't shut up about my trips, and my colleagues started to get curious. After some urging, Lonely Planet put 'dark sky travel' on its list of top travel trends for 2019, and that same year, I re-entered the freelance world and applied to become one of DarkSky International's official 'delegates' – individuals who have agreed to be a local point of contact, submit annual reports and use our particular skills to help fight light pollution.

Then, of course, in 2020, the pandemic hit and every person on Earth found themselves stuck at home at the same time. I couldn't get out of London to see a truly starry sky, so I started leading people on Twitter in quarantine stargazing sessions with the hashtag #Starentine. Each week, I would point out a familiar night-sky object, like the bright star Sirius or the constellation Orion. This got a bit of media attention, and I was soon joined by people all over the world, from Kazakhstan to Australia and Brazil to Vermont; we were finding our way through a difficult time, online together under the stars. For many who participated, it was their first time truly understanding light pollution, but despite the community we had built,

I couldn't find anyone in London working on the problem. It seemed like I was operating as an island – the lone, insane darkness-seeker in an oceanic city. So, I founded a community group called Dark Sky London, with the remit of 'rewilding the night'. Since then, Dark Sky London has held stargazing events in south London, taken night walks to experience darkness in Epping Forest, conducted street light audits with local political parties, and worked with organisations like Buglife, The Countryside Charity (CPRE) and the Royal Astronomical Society to campaign the government for better national policies against light pollution.

There is no national body that governs street lighting in Britain. Instead it is regulated by local councils or town committees, and there are a great many varieties of lighting across the country. There is also, it turns out, no official list of towns in the UK *without* street lighting, according to the National Association of Local Councils. I put out a call on social media and was staggered by the impassioned responses. Everyone, it seemed, was keen to talk about their dark home village, reveal one just over the hill that resists lighting, or boast about one they discovered on holiday. I started a spreadsheet and quickly added up the names of more than fifty villages and settlements sourced from my social posts alone. There must be hundreds more.

I wanted to see what one of these places was like. So, on a winter morning, I went to visit my friend and fellow travel journalist Lottie Gross in her village of Brightwell-cum-Sotwell* in Oxfordshire.

Lottie collected me at Didcot Parkway, where the sun was out, the sky clear and the station empty. She was waiting behind a line of taxis in her little grey Ford Fiesta with her sassy Manchester terrier, Milo, buckled into a harness.

We drove a few minutes up the road to her childhood home: a semi-detached, 1960s red-brick house in a row of other red-brick houses across from a small green. Her mum, Helen, was curled up on a big couch when we came in, and immediately hugged me and rushed into the kitchen to put the kettle on.

When I asked why Brightwell has no street lights, Helen told me it's always been that way.

'Every few years, it comes back up for debate with the village council, and every time it's rejected. People here just don't want street lights.'

I asked why.

'People like the darkness, they like to be able to see the stars,' she said. 'No one wants street lights glaring into their windows at night, either. They think it will disrupt their sleep. But mainly it's for the peace and quiet – the feeling of being in a village in the countryside, not a big city.'

---

* 'Cum', which is a Latin word meaning 'plus' or 'along with', was popularly used as a place-naming convention at a certain point in British history, especially when two adjacent villages or parishes were combined. This was the case when the villages of Brightwell and Sotwell were joined together as one civil parish in 1948.

For many people, including me, flipping on a lamp at night is almost as basic as breathing, while the idea of walking down a dark street with no street lights and no torch is an uncomfortable prospect. Several studies, including research by Transport for London in 2011 and a 2017 report by the Essex Police, have found no evidence that turning street lights off at night causes an increase in crime, accidents or anti-social behaviour. But an unlit alley persistently conjures images of lurking violence waiting in the shadows. We believe that we are more in danger at night, a construct that I thought might trace back to a time when humans were preyed upon by fierce nocturnal animals and nighttime was, in fact, more dangerous. And yet here I was in a community that had actively chosen to live this way.

Later that afternoon, Lottie and I went for a walk up the Wittenham Clumps, the wonderfully named pair of chalk hills that rise almost 400 metres above the surrounding countryside. We climbed the larger of the two, Round Hill, dodging a few wandering cows and many of their dung pats, and stood next to the crowning copse, planted in the 1740s, which is said to have the oldest beech trees in England. There we watched as the sun dropped below the horizon to the southwest, leaving a layer cake of pink and orange sky perfectly free of clouds. Behind us, the waxing gibbous moon was rising over the hill to the east, the site of an Iron Age fort. It's no stretch to imagine that humans have been watching the sun's daily descent from this spot for 2,000 years. Apart from the grey cooling towers of Didcot

Power Station that now interrupt the view, not much has changed about this experience for millennia.

That night, when it was fully dark, Lottie and I walked from her home down the unlit footpath that connects her street to the village centre, for dinner at the Red Lion, a sixteenth-century timber pub that stands on the historic boundary line between the villages of Brightwell and Sotwell.

'I already feel freaked out. How is it so dark!' Lottie laughed as we stumbled along – she wasn't used to walking this path without a torch. It was indeed very dark, and the walk was short, so our eyes did not have the necessary twenty minutes to fully adjust before we reached the pub. In a way, we were walking blind. Off to our right, branches in the hedge made a low scratching noise in the wind. We both jumped. I tried to play it cool – I was supposed to be the darkness guru, after all – but in truth, being outside in the woods at night without a torch can be scary.

Emerging at the end of the footpath was a relief. A warming glow seeped out from the curved windows of the pub, welcoming us in much the same way that inns have for centuries: as places where weary travellers could find a roaring fire, a bed, a meal, a tipple and shelter from the cold, dark winter.

Back in London, inspired by my visit to Brightwell, I decided to time-travel. The practical matter of lighting our way at night to avoid tripping over tree roots and bumping into darkened foliage is as old as settled human civilisation. Romans, rather than installing lanterns, which would need to be lit by hand each night, instead employed a slave, known as a lanternarius, to carry a torch or oil lamp to light the way. This system was used in many places, including London, where, from medieval times until the eighteenth century, the city's wealthy employed 'link-boys' with torches to light them through the urban laneways, and the exteriors of grander homes had an iron funnel-shaped cap that was used to extinguish the torch on the doorstep – a few of these can still be seen on Georgian homes today. Samuel Pepys and Charles Dickens both mentioned link-boys in their writings about London, and according to the *1811 Dictionary of the Vulgar Tongue*, in thieves' cant, a dialect used by criminals, linkboys were known as 'glym jack' ('glym' meant 'light') or 'moon-curser' because their services were not required on moonlit nights.

I wanted to get a real sense of what London might've been like at night back then, so I signed up for a twilight walking tour put on by the playhouse Shakespeare's Globe. The website promised to 'invoke the absolute darkness of the sixteenth century and discover where Shakespeare's fascination with night might have come from'. From the ghostly ramparts of *Hamlet* to the moonlit realms of *A Midsummer Night's Dream*, many of Shakespeare's plays evoke night or darkness. As tour guide Michael walked us along the South Bank at sunset, he explained that the area south of the River Thames was, in Shakespeare's time, free land outside of the Puritan control of the City of London to the north. People came across the river in small ferries or skiffs to what was essentially a red-light district offering all sorts of nocturnal excitement forbidden on the other bank: theatre, pubs, brothels and arenas for the cruel spectator sport of the day, animal baiting.

'This whole area would have been absolutely pitch black,' Michael said, pointing to the now-banked and paved walkway along the river. 'It would have been muddy. Boggy. Absolutely dark and dank and slippery. There was a curfew of nine p.m. on the other side, so if you missed the last ferry home, you might be stuck sleeping rough or out in muddy farmland.' As Michael told us, even in the more regulated City of London, life continued to be dangerous and difficult after dark, from uneven footing to robberies.

One place that gives a dramatic sense of what the city was like before electric light is Dennis Severs' House, a four-storey, red-brick home on a cobbled street behind Spitalfields Market in east London. The house dates to the 1720s and fell into disrepair before it was bought in 1979 by a bohemian and artist named Dennis Severs. Severs turned it into a living museum depicting the life of a fictional eighteenth-century family. When Severs died in 2000, *Guardian* writer Gavin Stamp wonderfully described him as, 'one of those Americans in England who seemed to have arrived from nowhere, to have no past, no roots and who, so irritatingly, could not be placed socially'. Severs was an eccentric who spent years living in and working on the derelict house, turning it into an evocative place of pre-electric atmosphere that would, as he put it, 'get the twenty-first century out of your eyes and ears'.

When I visited on a cold March night, the cobblestones of Folgate Street were glistening from the evening's rain. There was nothing on the exterior of the house to indicate the museum, so I stood and waited in front of a big, black door at Number 18 and hoped for the best. Flickering in soft orange above the door was a vintage gas lamp – one of only a few thousand left in the whole of London.

London was one of the first cities in the world to have street lights; its laneways were illuminated by fixed fire torches as early as the sixteenth century, and then, in 1807, the first gas street lamps were installed along Pall Mall near Buckingham Palace, trialled by German inventor Frederick Winsor. Westminster Bridge was lit up two years later, and numerous towns across Britain and Europe followed suit. Gas lamps became the gold standard for decades, at first lit by an army of lamplighters and later fitted with clockwork controllers that ignited a pilot burner at a set time each day.

When experiments with electricity started to prove useful, electric arc lamps were introduced in the 1870s as a trial in Los Angeles, and in Paris and London soon after. Electric Avenue in Brixton, south London, was the first shopping street in the world to have electric lighting, installed in cast-iron Victorian canopies that were damaged during the Second World War and later removed.

In Gateshead, British inventor Joseph Swan lit his own home with his early version of an electric lamp, and in 1879, Mosley Street in nearby Newcastle-upon-Tyne became the first road lit with Swan's incandescent lightbulbs. In 1881, Swan lit up London's Savoy Theatre, which became the world's first public building illuminated entirely by electricity.

Electric light acts like a relentless, inexhaustible flood. A study carried out at Texas A&M University tested how far away the human eye could see a candle flame. To calculate the distance, they compared the relative brightness of candle flames and stars and determined that a candle flame could be seen by human eyes up to 2.76 kilometres away at the farthest. Compare that to light from LEDs, which can travel 30 or 40 kilometres, and the cumulative skyglow from a big city, which can sometimes be seen 200 kilometres away.

While I was waiting under the gas lamp at Dennis Severs' House, an urban fox trotted by, no doubt having scoured the bins at nearby Spitalfields Market for remnants of the bao buns and designer doughnuts consumed by the day's visitors. The London Wildlife Trust estimates that the city has a stable population of around 10,000 urban foxes. Wander around at night and you will likely spot one darting across a road or into a back garden, or be awoken by the violent shrieks of a vixen letting males in the area know she is seeking a mate. The foxes' presence is a ghostly reminder that the city somehow lives, breathes and produces wild life – nocturnal life – below its faceless mass of brick, concrete and glass. I pulled out my phone and posted a video captioned 'Life is still wild in the City of London'.

Finally, Dennis Severs' black door opened, and a staff member introduced herself in a whisper as Lisa. She reminded me and a French family who had also turned up that this was a silent tour and to please respect the rules set out by Mr Severs: there should be no speaking, phone use or noisemaking during our visit.

Inside, the hush fell like a blanket and my eyes adjusted to the low light of candles as I descended to the basement, which was made up to look like the family kitchen. There were the sounds of a ticking clock, far-off bells, the rumble of a tube train somewhere below, the gentle rattle of porcelain dishware on an antique cabinet and the creak of wooden floorboards as I stepped carefully around a table covered in flickering candles and bowls of real fruit. A small sign rested on the table:

> *Shh! What you hear and smell*
> *is very much a part of the whole*
> *picture as anything you see.*

I inhaled and caught the ligneous scent of firewood from a log burner that also served as the kitchen's cooker.

Severs wanted the house to be alive, to evoke the feeling as you enter each room that a member of the family has left just moments before. Food is half-eaten on plates; goblets of wine sit waiting to be finished; fires glow; the smell of gardenia perfume wafts through the bedroom as if the unseen lady of the house has just sprayed it seconds before. At moments, I felt dizzy from the atmosphere, like ghosts were near.

The cellar was a dark, sod-floor room next to the kitchen. There were no lights, so I was completely blind walking in from the candlelight next door. Lisa told me later that when the museum first opened, Severs led tours himself, locking visitors in the cellar with the lights off for twenty minutes at the start.

'People complained that it was too dark to see,' she said, 'but Mr Severs felt that what you couldn't see would be filled in by your imagination.' He believed that a total lack of exposure to artificial light was necessary to properly immerse people into a different age.

After forty-five minutes in the house, slowly ascending from the cellar to the attic, I felt as if I'd really travelled through time. The scent of smoke mixed with mildew lingered in my nose. My body felt relaxed and sleepy from the candlelight, and I half expected to see an old horse-drawn coach pass by outside.

Instead, I stepped onto chilly Folgate Street into the LED light of the faux-Victorian street lamps, which were exceedingly bright. Looming over the street was the tower at 201 Broadgate, a skyscraper that now marks the end of old east London and the beginning of the financial district.

It was past 7 p.m. but lights were still blazing from many of its empty floors – bright white ghosts of office workers long gone home for the day.

I was standing at the spot where the gas lamps of historic London meet the glass towers and ubiquitous bright lights that are altering our planet in unimaginable ways.

2

FAMILY

New Zealand

On the last day of the year, I stood and looked up at Orion the Hunter in a grove of trees near the bottom of the South Island of New Zealand. It was the opening night of the annual Whare Flat Folk Festival, and my dad – a musician – had just finished playing his set. It had been several years since we'd last seen each other, and I was feeling nostalgic listening to his original songs. We were packing up the guitar cases into his little hatchback car under a sky that was inky black with fast-moving clouds clearing away to reveal thousands of stars.

'Did you find Orion?' Dad asked. I felt like a kid again, my dad showing me the stars in the sky, only this time we were somewhere very far away from the high desert of New Mexico. And Orion was upside down.

'I think so,' I hesitated. 'Are those three stars his belt?'

'Yep,' he said. 'And the cluster on the right pointing upwards is his sword. Pretty weird seeing him from down here, eh?' He grinned. Even after two decades, he still loved to take any chance to bask in having become a New Zealander.

Whare Flat is the oldest folk-music festival in New Zealand, first staged in 1975. It is held in a dreamy setting at Waiora Scout Camp, a 1940s campground in the Silver Stream Valley northwest of Dunedin, the city where Dad has lived for going on twenty years. The camp is tucked into a grove of tall pines and kānuka trees alongside the Silver Stream, a river called Whakaehu, meaning 'to scatter', in the Indigenous Māori language. A lovely word that also seemed to depict what I was seeing in the spray of stars around Orion – hundreds more than I'd ever seen in London – all framed by the whorling branches of the camp's tall conifers.

In the Southern Hemisphere, Orion and other constellations, as well as the Moon, appear upside down – at least to a visitor from the Northern Hemisphere. Imagine a constellation as a projection onto the sky, and two people are standing on a sphere viewing it from different angles. Orion, the famed hunter with his gleaming belt of stars, stands upright in England, but here he seems to cartwheel across the Kiwi sky, his feet in the air.

Dad has always had a wandering spirit. As a young hippie in the 1960s, he would hop on railway boxcars and ride as far as he could in any direction. In 1974, he set an incredible precedent for our family travel tradition by riding his horse, Gizmo, across the United States from California to Virginia, starting and ending at opposite coasts. It took seven months, and they travelled 4,000 miles, a story he recounts in his own book, *Man and Horse: The Long Ride Across America*.

Far-reaching journeys run in our veins, and perhaps because of that, we both chose lives outside of our home country. We also somehow ended up in the two places on the planet that are farthest apart from one another, where even the constellations are different.

New Zealand is antipodal to Britain, a mathematical and geographical term for two places that are located at diametrically opposite spots on a sphere. If it were physically possible to bore a hole straight through the centre of the planet, the antipode is where you'd pop out on the other side – hence 'the Antipodes', from Greek, 'feet opposite ours', an older nickname for Australia and New Zealand coined by early British colonists.

To really learn about the night, I knew I would have to begin at the beginning, which meant listening to and learning Indigenous knowledge and traditions of the dark and the stars. Long before Europeans set sail in their ships with their sights set on expansion, First Peoples around the world had developed rich traditions of sky study for navigation, time-tracking and spirituality. Theirs is the foundational human science of the night sky, remembered with care over thousands of years through traditional storytelling, ancient artwork on rocks and caves, and in song, dance and artisanship. I had come to see Dad and to view the stars in his chosen home down under while learning about the rich astronomical heritage of the Māori.

The Māori were skilled sailors who began navigating across Polynesia and the South Pacific around 1500 CE in all sorts of vessels, from small canoes to giant ships up to 40 metres long. They maintained a sophisticated knowledge of astronomy, weather, atmospheric conditions and seasons, which informed their te kapehu whetū or 'star compass': a system that divided the 360-degree ocean view around a boat into sections corresponding to four directions. Navigators used these sections to check where certain stars, the Moon and Sun rose and set on the horizon.

Skylore, astronomy and darkness are common themes in Kiwi culture, from the national icon, the silver fern – a plant whose underleaves reflect moonlight and helped Māori people find their way at night – to a 'sort of national obsession with the colour black', as Dad put it, reminding me that the name of the beloved national rugby team is the All Blacks. New Zealand has also made headlines in recent years with its attempt to become the world's first 'dark sky nation', a plan that would see it have more land area than any other country protected from light pollution, as well as national legislation against it. At the time of my trip, 'dark sky nation' was not a designation that DarkSky International had ever given out, so I was writing a feature about it for the organisation's magazine, *Nightscape*. I scheduled interviews with local advocates and planned a father-daughter trip to the South Island's huge Aoraki Mackenzie International Dark Sky Reserve to experience the Kiwi nights for myself.

My journey to Dad had started on Christmas Eve – a ten-hour flight from London to Texas followed by a fourteen-hour long-haul to Auckland, crossing over the International Date Line and skipping Christmas Day entirely. A final two-hour leg to the South Island would land me in Dunedin, where Dad and my stepmum, Kathryn, would pick me up.

Navigating across the world is now done via GPS: the Global Positioning System, a US-owned set of thirty-one satellites that orbit Earth. Together with three other sets of satellites owned by Russia, the EU and China, they form the global navigation satellite systems. The blue dot showing your spot on a mapping app is a signal from a satellite pinging your phone to triangulate where you are.

But GPS was only deployed in the 1990s. For most of human history, people have navigated using natural cues like landmarks and the stars. And GPS satellites aren't the only orbiters in the sky. Several thousand satellites now fly at speed around Earth in low orbit – mostly science satellites measuring the atmosphere, environmental changes, weather and light pollution. But there are also an alarming number of commercial satellites being launched by unregulated private companies, many of them creating new light pollution as their metal surfaces reflect the Sun's light back to the ground in bright sprays that cut across telescopes and images that astronomers use to study the cosmos.

It was after midday on Boxing Day when I finally reached Dunedin Airport. Dad was waiting for me outside the terminal wearing his standard uniform of a faded western shirt, worn-out Wrangler jeans and Converse Chuck Taylor low-tops, which he has dozens of in every colour, some self-dyed. He gave me a long-awaited big hug, and after shedding a few tears, we stepped out together into the midday sun. It was a week past the summer solstice and the Southern Hemisphere warmth was a shock after the frigid December temperatures in London and Houston. I pulled out my sunglasses.

Dad, Kathryn and I spent the Christmas break quietly at their home in Port Chalmers, a peninsular village north of the city of Dunedin. Kathryn had started chemotherapy the month before, so we were in resting mode. The combination of summer and Christmas was strange for me. Instead of hot chocolate and fuzzy blankets, we made gin and tonics and sat under a sky-blue umbrella in the garden with the hiss of grasshopper wings breaking the warm silence, and their two cats, Harriet and Gidget, stalking through the tall grass hunting flies.

One evening, we migrated to the front of the house where there was a lounge chair for Kathryn, who despite feeling unwell, was always dressed up in colourful patterned tops, scarves and antique jewellery – all of which she also sold through her local boutique, Frills and Folly. I sat on the steps next to her, stroking Gidget, who purred and stretched her calico belly out on the paving stones, soaking up every inch of afternoon warmth. As we watched the sunset, Kathryn told me in her matter-of-fact way about her chemo treatments and shared her favourite New Zealand word: whānau. Whānau, she explained, is the Māori term for 'extended family' and can also be used to describe your community or chosen family.

'We wouldn't be getting through all this without our whānau,' she said, describing how their local friends had rallied to help with her treatment. When they first moved to New Zealand, Dad was studying for his master's degree in music at the University of Otago (he went on to retire as a tenured professor) and he and Kathryn fell in immediately with the local folk music club, where they found a crew of good friends. We agreed that having whānau is crucial when you're living far from home and family, and what I didn't realise at that moment was that I was in the process of building my own new whānau of night lovers through the writing of this book.

The sunset fell around us in soft pinks and a fresh fog lifted up off the harbour, swirling itself into new clouds around the green hills to the west. Kathryn eventually went in, and I lingered outside a little longer and watched the stars come out in the back garden, sparkling on the glassy waters of the harbour far below.

*

A few days later, Dad and I packed a few essentials into the car and set out for the South Island's great interior. We were bound for Lake Tekapo, the village at the centre of the Aoraki Mackenzie International Dark Sky Reserve.* Covering a vast 4,300-square-kilometre section of the South Island, the reserve is home to the University of Canterbury's astronomical research centre, Mount John Observatory, as well as Dark Sky Project, an 'astrotourism' experience owned by the Ngāi Tahu, one of the main Māori communities, called iwi. When Aoraki Mackenzie was designated a Dark Sky Reserve in 2012, it was the largest one in the world. Outdoor lighting controls had first been put into place here in the 1980s to limit light pollution for the astronomical observatory. There was also the hope that the measures would conserve energy, protect wildlife and bring in visitors for stargazing.

Dark Sky Project was the area's first nighttime visitor experience. It began as a project called Earth & Sky when astronomy advocates Hide Ozawa and Graeme Murray, who were helping to install a telescope at Mount John, began campaigning to protect the area's natural darkness. They were joined by other influential folks around

---

* Dark Sky Reserves, Parks, Sanctuaries and Communities all over the world are certified by DarkSky International (formerly the International Dark-Sky Association). Similar to the UNESCO World Heritage programme, these preserves must meet a stringent set of requirements to maintain their status, including measurable levels of darkness, shielded light fixtures and community involvement. They must submit annual reports to prove these ongoing protections.

the region, including Steve Butler from the Department of Conservation and former MP Margaret Austin, who helped lead the charge for Dark Sky Reserve status. Earth & Sky then partnered with the tourism office of the Ngāi Tahu, the largest Māori iwi in the South Island. Together, they opened Dark Sky Project, offering stargazing tours at the observatory, to which they had been granted exclusive access. In 2019, with Ngāi Tahu investment, they added a massive visitor centre by the lake with a scale model of the solar system so big that Pluto touched the shore, as well as a permanent home for the Victorian Brashear Telescope, an 1894 brass masterpiece built in Pennsylvania and moved to New Zealand for research in the 1960s.

We drove up the east coast following a portion of State Highway 1, the longest road in New Zealand. It spans both islands from top to bottom, connected by ferry across the Cook Strait. Dad told me that musicians can ride the ferry for free by playing for their passage, and recounted a time when he'd done it, pulling out his guitar and playing a few bluegrass tunes in exchange for a ticket to ride.

Near Shag Point, we hugged the ocean, where huge Pacific waves were crashing in white foam and sea mist hovered over the highway. In Oamaru, we made a pit stop for coffee and fuel. This was an area settled by Māori people from at least the 1100s. In February 1770, Captain James Cook landed nearby in the *Endeavour*, and the town was founded later, in 1858, by the colonial civil engineer

John Turnbull Thomson, who named all of the streets after British rivers. We parked at the corner of Wansbeck and Tyne Streets and walked around the Victorian Precinct, a cluster of nineteenth-century buildings constructed of local limestone.

At the top of Tyne Street was a converted grain elevator with a rusting steam locomotive in front and, off to one side, a small zeppelin had been hung up. Dad pointed out a sign that said: 'Steampunk HQ'.

'Gotta love these crazy Kiwis,' he laughed affectionately. Oamaru was a sleepy farming town until 2016, when local residents held the world's largest steampunk gathering – a feat that was recorded as a Guinness World Record. Local shops and galleries embraced the nineteenth-century sci-fi vibe and now the steampunk festival is held every June.

From Oamaru, we cut west along Highway 83, following the Waitaki River inland. The uplands began to rise from the coast in brown brushstroke mountains shadowed by puffs of cloud. We were entering Mackenzie Country and the Riddermark – the setting for the horse kingdom of Rohan in Peter Jackson's *The Lord of the Rings* films – wide, sepia-hued plains set below the soaring Southern Alps, which stand in majestically for the fictional Misty Mountains of Middle Earth.

The Mackenzie Country is striking and difficult to forget – a cinematic landscape in every sense, and if you've seen the films, this may well be *the* lasting image of Middle

Earth in your mind. It is for me. These lands are defined by a series of narrow alpine lakes formed into ice-blue fingers by receding glaciers. Their colour is a heavenly, milky blue, caused by a fine silt of eroded bedrock in the water. It's a blue that seems more opaque than the sky, like the blue of turquoise stone.

By early afternoon, we rolled up over a gentle crest and the township of Lake Tekapo came into view, a small collection of black-frame cottages – 'All these houses are black,' mused Dad, 'the obsession continues' – and a single strip of cafés and restaurants along the lake, which was an aqua blue so bright it seemed to glow in the midday sunshine. Our holiday cottage along the lake's edge was all cedarwood inside and had a collection of 1990s furniture – light wood chairs upholstered in faded geometric fabric, a shaggy beige rug, and a maple coffee table with peeling moisture rings. There was a sliding door leading onto a deck overlooking the lake, ringed by snowy mountains. Ours was the last house before the shore – the only thing standing between it and the water was a tiny stone chapel called the Church of the Good Shepherd, built in the 1930s and a feature in many photos of Lake Tekapo.

Once we'd settled in, we wandered to the shore, where a rocky beach met the shock of blue water, and we had a laugh at dozens of piles of stone cairns left along the waterline by visitors.

'People,' chuckled Dad. 'Always have to leave their mark. These things are so silly and, in that way, kind of amazing when you think about it. The human urge to leave something behind – some sign we were here.'

I didn't disagree, but it made me consider the marks we make on our environment. It's difficult to deny the fact that, out of all the life forms on Earth, humans seem to be in some way a special species in our consciousness, self-awareness and ability to communicate and create technology, music and art.

But don't birds also make music?

And don't hydrogen and oxygen atoms by themselves collide and freeze into ice crystals that paint the sunsets onto the sky?

From the top of Mount John, it feels as though the entire universe is visible. The mountain juts up over Tekapo, out of a bowl of prairie that's surrounded on all sides by the Southern Alps. The mountains stretch away in brushstrokes of slate grey, cobalt and stone blue, and the night falls in an ombré blush of pink and violet that fades dark to reveal the cosmos.

The sun was just going down when we set out for the mountaintop with Adrien Vilquin-Barrajon in his little car. Adrien is the guiding operations manager at Dark Sky Project, and he lives in Lake Tekapo. Born in Paris, Adrien speaks fast, with a self-assured French accent, and he drove fast, too, up the winding road to Mount John Observatory, all the while explaining life in the small tourist town and what it's like to lead visitors through the Southern Hemisphere skies every night.

'A large part of what we do is making sure people

understand the Māori traditions and sky knowledge that came before European colonists arrived,' he said. 'All of our guides are trained in Māori stories, and we spent a lot of time with Māori knowledge-holders when we designed the visitor experience. That involved learning not just the different constellations that Māori people see in the sky, but also how those affect all parts of life.' He turned onto a steep road that switchbacked up the mountainside.

When we got halfway up, he turned off the car's headlights. 'Sorry about this,' he said. 'We have to turn off all the lights because the astronomers are working tonight and lights completely ruin their observations. Don't worry, I've done this many times.' He grinned but I was not reassured and kept a nervous eye on the little road, and the sheer drop from the passenger's side window down the dark cliff.

It was cold and windy at the top, and there were no trees, so you could see for miles in every direction. Above, the sun had almost disappeared, and the world was a dome of purple sky. Below, the town of Tekapo was a crescent of amber lights along the lakeshore. Adrien led us up a small flight of stairs to a café where the lights were off and faux candles provided minimal illumination. As my eyes adjusted, mountains started appearing in shadowy outlines beyond the lake. With the horizon line well below us, it felt like we were swimming in the sky. It made me breathless.

We were joined that night by a group of public visitors arriving all together in a minibus, and I was suddenly grateful to have been driven up the mountainside in Adrien's car rather than a bus with its lights off. It had got dark very quickly. The purple hue disappeared from the sky and, with no moon up, we had to tread carefully along the pathways that led between the café and the observatory rooms, which were spaced around the top of the peak.

We stood outside in a semi-circle while a guide named Heather introduced herself, then led the group through a Māori acknowledgement ceremony in which she named and thanked the ancestors and recognised them as the tangata whenua, or original inhabitants of Aotearoa. She explained that the ancestors were the keepers of tātai arorangi – the Māori astronomical knowledge that informed everything from growing crops to navigation, fishing and the calendar.

'When Māori people look up into the night sky, they see more than just stars and planets,' she said. 'They see a connection to their ancestors and all life. Māori people used the sky as a kind of life map, which marked places, time and seasons, helped to predict the weather, to know when certain fish were abundant and when to plant crops.' She then recounted the story of how the stars were born:

'There was a legendary warrior named Tamarereti, who was once sailing his waka, a type of canoe, far out on a lake, quite like the one below us now. He was very far from home and night began to fall. At that time, there were no stars in the sky, and the night was completely dark. Tamarereti felt he was in danger from a lake monster called the taniwha, so he made the decision to ascend from the lake and fly his waka home through the sky. As he sailed, he scattered glowing stones along the way, leaving a bright wake behind. Today, we call this glowing trail the Milky Way and those stones are the stars.'

Next, she asked us to close our eyes for a few moments. We stood quietly and then opened them all at once to reveal the sky utterly filled with stars.

'Can you see the Milky Way?'

A few people gasped and a lady next to me spoke up in a North American accent to say she'd never seen our galaxy before. Heather explained that, because of light pollution, most people can't see the Milky Way any more. 'That's why the Dark Sky Reserve regulations are so important here – to protect the darkness and our access to the night sky.'

'So from now on,' she continued, 'if you look up and see the Milky Way, you will think of Tamarereti and remember how the stars were scattered in the sky. And if you don't see the Milky Way, you will remember what can be lost.'

The Māori are among many Indigenous peoples, including Aboriginal Australians, Native Americans, Tibetans, Guaraní and Maya, who have maintained extensive knowledge of the night sky over millennia. They use the stars as cues for activities fundamental to existence, including planting and harvesting food, travelling, hunting and spiritual rituals.

As Earth slowly orbits the Sun over a year, what we see in the night sky changes. Indigenous peoples noticed that certain constellations would appear at certain times of the year, and so would use them as sky landmarks for the change of seasons. For example, ancient Egyptians noticed that the star Sirius – the brightest in the night sky – was first visible in the east just before sunrise in August. This would occur right before the annual flooding of the Nile, and so Sirius came to mark the start of their harvest season.

Dr Rangi Mātāmua, a Māori scholar working to reclaim Indigenous astronomy as part of a continued process of decolonisation, shows how knowledge of the stars was embedded into the Māori language and even the landscapes of Aotearoa. In his book *Matariki: The Star of the Year*, he writes:

> When the first European settlers arrived to Aotearoa in the late 1700s and early 1800s, they were astounded by the large amount of astronomical knowledge maintained by Māori. It was widely recognised that Māori knew much more about the night sky than their European counterparts, and their ability to observe distant nebula and other objects with their naked eye was unequalled. However, colonisation and its many attributes infiltrated to the core of Māori society, affecting all cultural practices, including Māori astronomy.

In the West, many of us take the well-known constellations, such as Orion – one of our most recognisable star patterns – as a given. But these are cultural constructs. Humans have been telling stories about the different patterns and pictures they see in the stars for millennia, and those pictures differ across cultures and time.

The Aboriginal peoples of Australia, who are now accepted as the world's first astronomers, have a practice of 'sky knowledge' going back to 8000 BCE – several millennia before the Babylonians, who began practising astronomy around 2000 BCE. The ancient Egyptians also kept detailed records of the night sky some 4,000 or 5,000 years ago, enshrined as hieroglyphs in the painted tombs of the pharaohs in the Nile Valley. The Maya created extensive astronomical calendars, made spiritual predictions and built storied temples according to astronomical alignments. Some of the earliest Native American peoples also built great cities designed according to the movements of the sky, like the one at Chaco Canyon in what is now New Mexico, built around 900 CE by the Ancestral Puebloans. They recorded significant astronomical events in petroglyphs, including solar eclipses and what some archeoastronomers believe might be an eleventh-century supernova: an ancient painting of an exploding star. The Skidi Band of the Pawnee People, who live in what is now the US Midwest, saw a 'council of chiefs' in the stars, which represented their governing elders.

Before setting off for New Zealand, I'd joined a series of workshops on Indigenous astronomy organised by Annette Lee, a Lakota astronomer and founder of Native Skywatchers, an initiative that is recording, mapping and sharing Indigenous star knowledge. During one session, Nancy Maryboy and David Begay, elders from the Diné (Navajo) Nation in the southwest US, shared how the stars align with their four sacred mountains surrounding Diné lands. They also explained that, according to Diné culture, many of the sky stories are 'Winter Stories' that are only supposed to be recounted during the winter months. Together, Maryboy and Begay wrote *Seeing the Skies Through Navajo Eyes*, in which they share Diné astronomy, including the constellations as seen by Navajo knowledge-holders.

One story, the 'Sparkling Seeds', concerns the star cluster Dilyéhé, which is known in Western astronomy as the Pleiades – the tornado of sister-stars that I love. In the story, Dilyéhé takes the form of a group of boys, running over a hill beyond their parents' view – this is when Dilyéhé sets, disappearing from the night sky. The boys symbolise 'sparkling' corn seeds, disappearing as they are planted. So corn planting should begin when the constellation Dilyéhé, or the Pleiades, sets in late April.

The Pleiades is present in many Indigenous astronomy traditions and known by many names in different cultures. The Māori people call it Matariki, and its reappearance around early July marks the start of the Māori new year. Traditional celebrations involve several nights of viewing the Pleiades, as well as mourning the deceased who have gone to live in the stars and offering food to the celestia, who have welcomed the ones who passed over. Like many elements of Māori culture, the observance of Matariki declined in the nineteenth century with the dominance of European settlers. But thanks to the work of Professor Mātāmua and other Māori activists, strides have been made in recent decades to revive and honour Māori traditions, and in 2022, Matariki was celebrated as a public holiday in New Zealand for the first time.

Back on Mount John, Heather quietly asked the group to focus on the sky in silence for a few moments, taking in the Large and Small Magellanic Clouds – two of the only nearby galaxies that can be seen with the unaided eye. They are only visible from the Southern Hemisphere, and it was my first time seeing them. They appeared as two smudges, almost like a fingerprint had been wiped across glass and blurred the stars. It was incredible to think that each of these tiny smudges was another galaxy containing some 30 billion stars and trillions of planets.

Then Heather asked if there were any Australians in the group, and a couple of people raised their hands. Using a green laser pointer, she indicated a dark patch in the gleaming band of the Milky Way.

'This is the head of the Great Emu,' she explained, circling what looked like a large beak. 'A constellation revered by many Aboriginal Australian societies.' Where later European astronomers told stories about their gods by connecting the outlines of stars, a number of Indigenous communities instead saw pictures in the dark patches *between* the stars. Heather explained that, for many Aboriginal peoples, the Emu is the single most recognisable image in the night sky – a constellation entirely defined by the dark.

*

While Indigenous peoples each held their own unique cosmological belief systems, there were some common themes. Namely, the interconnected relationships of all living things, from animals, birds and fish to water, plants, clouds, winds and thunder, and the invisible beings of dreams and the imagination – a holistic way of looking at life lost by Western civilisations.

Colonialism, spurred by the extractive nature of capitalism, has resulted in many Indigenous peoples, peoples of colour and societies in the Global South facing the violent and systematic eradication of systems of knowledge that have been the bedrock of a balanced life on Earth for millennia. These systems kept human beings intimately connected to both the Earth and the sky. Many Indigenous cultures, especially those enslaved, brutalised or forcibly assimilated by European colonisers, have lost their knowledge of the stars. Within Western astronomy, too, the contributions of Indigenous peoples have been ignored and devalued.

During one of the Indigenous astronomy sessions I'd joined, Anishinaabe artist and elder Carl Gawboy talked about a group of mysterious rock paintings near Hegman Lake, Minnesota, whose meanings were no longer known by his community. Gawboy spent decades studying them and deduced that they were Ojibwe depictions of the winter constellations: the Wintermaker, the Great Moose and the Great Panther. Gawboy said the paintings' meanings had been lost due to 'the forcible movement of the Ojibwe people to reservations, the boarding school era, and the whole reservation period, in which being free to travel to the rock painting sites was actually prohibited, so that this knowledge could not be continued on to the next generation'.

The two majestic Southern Hemisphere smudges I was seeing for the first time in New Zealand – the Magellanic Clouds – are named after the Portuguese navigator Ferdinand Magellan, who is often credited with 'discovering' them during the first voyage around the world in 1519. In reality, Magellan died trying violently to colonise the Philippines, and it was an enslaved Malay man named Enrique de Malaca who finished the expedition and was the first person to completely circumnavigate the Earth. Of course, people have known about the Magellanic Clouds for millennia – the earliest known depiction of them was captured in a prehistoric petroglyph in what is now Chile, and they may also have been observed by medieval Persians.

Heather next asked us to follow her down the darkened path to the observatories and their telescopes. In hushed tones, we climbed inside the red-lit domes and took turns looking through the viewfinders to see Saturn, with its rings of rock-and-ice debris, visible in incredible detail.

It was at this point that someone in the group got audibly excited. Something was moving in the sky outside – a bright, singular light floating unblinkingly across the expanse. There were murmurings about it being a UFO. Everyone poured outside to have a look.

'Definitely not aliens, sorry!' laughed Heather. 'In fact, that is a satellite. If we stand here long enough, you'll see dozens, if not hundreds, crossing the sky. They are everywhere now, and more are on the way. Elon Musk wants to put thousands of them up there.'

Satellites are used for more than airline navigation and Google Maps. There are now thousands orbiting Earth, providing scientific information about the climate, ecosystems, weather and communications, as well as serving purposes of geopolitical intelligence. They can monitor wildfires, facilitate long-distance phone calls and track the wildebeest migrations across the Serengeti. They also help us study the extent of light pollution.

But as with the rock cairns on the lakeshore, when too many add up, they become their own form of pollutant – a problem that has been increasing exponentially over the last few years. In 2018, there were only a few thousand operational satellites, run primarily for scientific purposes. But private satellite launches, and the use of space, are not regulated by any global governing body, and some companies have begun launching upwards of sixty satellites at a time. Given there is little or no governmental oversight, most of these satellites have been placed there without the consultation or input of Indigenous peoples or the wider public.

Much like plastics, satellites continue to exist long after their usefulness runs out. The new satellite 'megaconstellations', which are groups of sixty-plus launched in pearl-string formations, have relatively short lifespans of just three or four years, after which time they become space debris hovering above the atmosphere, waiting to collide with science satellites and even crewed spaceships. This is already happening. In 2019, the European Space Agency (ESA) had to move one of its scientific observation satellites so that it would not collide with one of Starlink's units. The International Space Station, similarly, often has to manoeuvre itself to avoid collisions with space debris. As of July 2024, the satellite-tracking website Orbiting Now listed 10,277 objects in various orbits around Earth. It's estimated that, if things continue this way, by 2030 there could be more than 100,000 satellites in orbit, most of which will be owned by private corporations, such as Elon Musk's telecommunications company, Starlink.

I'd earlier discussed this with Aparna Venkatesan, who argued that space should be considered a 'global commons', much like international waters. In a recent seminar on dark and quiet skies held by the International Astronomical Union, Dr Venkatesan spoke about how seeing human-made objects in the sky changes not only our sense of place but also the narratives that we will create about our existence and our view of the universe.

'It's not just about individual streaks [of light from satellites],' she said. 'With so many glinting bits of orbiting hardware above us, there is an aggregate effect of a rising background of light, which will lead to brightening night skies globally.' Because satellites orbit the whole planet, even

Dark Sky Reserves like Aoraki Mackenzie are not spared their effects. A fact we were seeing in real time over Mount John, as the UFO-like light trailed through the Dark Sky Reserve and through the images being captured by the telescopes that night.

Together with several experts, including astronomer and outspoken dark sky advocate Dr John Barentine, a working group has been formed to address the issues caused by satellite pollution, including impacts on astronomical sciences and Indigenous communities. The group is collaborating with governments, the UN and private satellite companies with the aim of putting better policies and regulations into place before it's too late.

As the clock pushed past 11 p.m., the visitors quieted and pulled their jackets tight against the wind. It was difficult to take our eyes off the sky, which was completely free of clouds. Stars sparkled all the way down to the horizon like a sweep of glitter over the mountains.

'It's really something, isn't it?' said Dad. He'd spent most of the evening quietly taking it all in and asking geeky questions about the telescopes that went beyond my technical interest. From somewhere in the darkness, Adrien appeared, and it was time to go. I took one last, long breath, knowing there was a chance I might not see this view again. I wanted to memorise it.

We were quiet as Adrien drove down the mountain. The night had settled over us and made everything softer and less urgent. It felt sacrilegious to interrupt such a reverent calm with any conversation. Back at the visitor centre, we thanked Adrien and wished him well, then drove to the cottage in the dark and fell into a deep, uninterrupted sleep.

Before heading home, we decided to visit Aoraki Mount Cook, New Zealand's highest peak, about 100 kilometres from Tekapo. From the mountain's base, trailheads lead trekkers deep into the national park and up the mountain, which juts more than 3,700 metres up in a perfect white triangle.

Setting off early in the morning, we took the only road into the village, a two-lane highway that followed the length of another perfect blue glacial lake, Lake Pukaki, its milky waters fed by the Tasman and Hooker Glaciers, which rest in the valleys near Mount Cook. Māori lore says that a great ancestor, Rākaihautū, dug out these lakes with a special stick called a kō and gave Pukaki its name, meaning 'bunched-up waters'.

We pulled off on the shoulder and stood in the empty road to snap a few pictures. We were tiny ants in a giant landscape swept into being by ancient ice.

'It's really something,' said Dad. And he was right. All of it – the sky, the glacier-carved stone, the ancestral stars and the radiant lakewater. All of it was alive with the stories of those who came before and our own new memories.

Learning to see the stars from the Māori perspective filled

me with hope. For them, the sky is a guide, a calendar and a cosmology: there is deep wisdom to learn if we are willing to listen.

3

Predators

Italy

There is a memory that looms large in my mind: a monumentally dark East African night and two yellow, glowing orbs shining through a tangle of *Commiphora* shrubs and tall grass.

'It's a leopard,' comes a whisper next to me. 'Young male leopard.'

The orbs disappear and reappear as the leopard blinks, and then the outlines of two rounded feline ears appear as safari guide Hamza Visram gently shines a torch over the bush, illuminating two golden eyeballs and a rippling coat of dark splotches.

This was not my first experience seeing a dangerous animal in the wild – it was not even my first experience on that particular trip to Tanzania. During the day we'd seen lions lazing on boulders warmed by the midday heat; hippos

soaking in river water, their ears flicking away flies; croco-
diles crawling up the rocky banks of the Mara River; even
a black mamba – Tanzania's deadliest and most mythologic-
ally charged snake – stretched across a deserted jeep track,
sunning itself. I had felt awe at seeing them – excited, even
intimidated. But I did not feel fear, exactly. It was daytime,
they were far away, and I was sitting comfortably in a safari
vehicle drinking a beer. Later, though, long after the sun
had set, poised there in the dark was a deadly predator with
murder mittens the size of my face, perfect night vision and,
presumably, an empty belly. And I *was* scared.

I had gone to Tanzania as part of a press trip with several
other journalists and the global brand director for Asilia
Africa, the safari company we were travelling with. I was
writing a story for the *South China Morning Post* about how
'citizen science' trips were a growing trend for African
safaris. Asilia had recently opened their newest location,
Usangu Expedition Camp, where we were staying, in the
less visited southern part of Tanzania. We were the only
guests.

I'd learned that citizen science safaris are intended to be
immersive experiences during which travellers are not just
passive watchers through jeep windows; instead, visitors get
involved with conservation science by, for example, placing
camera traps, learning to use triangulation equipment to
find the locations of collared lions, and cataloguing species
sightings and locations. On that night's drive, we were
using state-of-the-art, heat-sensing cameras connected to

mobile tablets, which allowed us to see and catalogue noc-turnal animals deep in the bush without resorting to the old-school and invasive method of shining giant spotlights out of the vehicle.

The leopard was not far away – about the distance of a large living room. And in an open-sided safari jeep with no windows or doors, there was very little between me and him. Earlier that night, when we'd departed from camp for the evening's drive, Hamza had climbed into the driver's seat and carefully placed a rifle on the dash, smiling. 'Just in case,' he said. This, I discovered, is standard practice on night game drives and daytime foot safaris in Tanzania – a violent fallback measure that is rarely, ideally not ever, called into use.

I am no stranger to guns. I was raised on a ranch in the New Mexico desert and taught to shoot a shotgun and a handgun when I was fourteen. Learning to shoot also meant learning how not to shoot: how to handle a gun so that no one got hurt; never to fire it straight up into the air lest the bullets rain back down on you; always to ensure the safety is on, and to hand it over with the barrel facing down. I learned every aspect of gun handling carefully, just as I learned how not to get kicked by a horse, how to change the oil in my car and how to drive a tractor. But from the moment I handled one, I hated everything about guns. The bang was horrific but worse was the gun's kickback, which travelled like an atomic shockwave through my whole body.

This is how we protect our people, our property, my

grandfather would say, and in that statement, he carried his entire family line – immigrants from England, his childhood of east Texas dirt poverty and the barefoot walk he made from his hometown towards the oil fields in the 1930s. Eventually, he worked his way to a dream: moving to New Mexico, buying a big tract of desert land and starting a ranch. He had known what it was to have nothing, not even an education, and to him, it must have seemed incomprehensible not to grip on to the life he'd built by any means necessary. *You never shoot at anyone unless they break into your house.* He tipped his cowboy hat back, cocked the pistol and fired, sending a tin can flying. Once I had learned to shoot and use a gun to his satisfaction, I vowed never to touch one again.

Seeing Hamza place the gun on the dash lifted memories out of my body – my ears rang with the pop of the rifle and a cold dread rinsed through me – and a feeling that I'd just done something that couldn't be undone. Once you squeeze the trigger, there are no take-backs. But Hamza's gentle smile was reassuring.

'We would never use this unless it were absolutely necessary,' he said.

Before we saw the leopard, we had eaten dinner under the branches of a huge, 800-year-old baobab tree, where the safari guides had hung tiny solar lights and built a fire, presumably having checked the surrounding bush for animals before setting up folding chairs and tables. The sun had gone down in a blaze of oranges and pinks, painting the level tops of the acacia trees until the stars came out and shone brightly through the canopy. We stood around the flames drinking gin.

Usangu Expedition Camp is located in a quiet part of Ruaha National Park. Unlike the Serengeti in northern Tanzania, which is busy day and night with photo-snapping safari-goers and rumbling 4x4s, deep in Ruaha, the animals are not habituated to the presence of people. Looking back now at my photos of that night, I see something I hadn't noticed at the time: in the background of almost every picture is a guide standing by the campfire with a rifle, its butt casually resting in the dirt, barrel pointed towards the Milky Way. They wanted us to feel safe and worry-free, but the truth was that we were intruders in very wild territory. When the sun went down and our scent carried on the soft evening breeze, a predator would have had every right to eat us for dinner. In that environment, it was a distinct possibility that we could become prey.

When I was a kid, I learned early to fear and respect wildlife. Our rural house was surrounded by desert creatures big and small. Almost all of my childhood pet cats were eaten by coyotes. My parents never sugar-coated this fact, the same way they let us learn about animal reproduction naturally when the dogs came into heat and let us watch when a foal was birthed in blood and corral dirt. They wanted my sister and me to know what was out there; what wildness was and how we were part of it. As soon as we could walk, we learned what to do if we saw a rattlesnake: to freeze, and not scream or run away, even if we wanted to.

I first encountered a wild snake aged seven. My family longed for a conventional backyard, but our attempts to lay grass and plant perennials simply did not take in the Santa Fe dust-soil. So, our 'backyard' was a patch of desert encircled by a brown adobe wall. On one side, my dad had built into the adobe an upright wagon wheel that formed a spoked window through the wall. One day I went outside looking for my cat and found her sitting in the wheel, staring down into a dead rose bush, tail swishing in that 'I've spotted something' way. I ran over to scoop her into my arms, but as I approached, I heard it.

Chkk chkk chkk chkk chkk chkk chkk chkk. The unmistakable, percussive clatter of a rattlesnake's tail; it was curled up in the rose bush. I did what I was taught: froze long enough to feel my heart pound in my little chest and blood thrum thick in my ears. Then one big step back. Another big, huge step back; grown-up-sized. A final giant step back. Then I ran, ran, ran into the house. Straight to Dad. *There's a rattlesnake*, I heaved. *A snake by the wall and the cat is looking at it.* Dad did what he had to do.

I feel bad that the snake had to die on my account. She was just living her snakey life. Probably hunting mice, having a nice sleep by the warm wall before heading over to our winter wood pile, where she'd find plenty of rodents to snack on.

As I got older, predators would come for our horses.

Mountain lions ventured down in the dark to the clusters of residences at the base of the mountains and found easy pickings in horse corrals and paddocks. I worked as an equestrian trainer in my twenties and, one night, my client's gelding was attacked by a mountain lion. The scene when I got there was gruesome: though left alive, the horse had huge, open claw marks down his neck exposing raw flesh. It was a violent moment I will never forget. It took weeks for the horse's wounds to heal and months for it to recover the muscle loss.

We'd been on our way back to the safari's main camp after dinner when Anderson, the guide driving the first vehicle, spotted the leopard in the bush and brought the caravan to a swift halt. The engines were shut off. The guides whispered into radios between the vehicles and everyone fell silent.

'Shh, quiet. Don't move, and don't talk,' they whispered to us urgently. Then the leopard stood and stalked forward a few feet in our direction. Hamza shifted soundlessly in the driver's seat. The leopard looked straight at me, and I felt my body kicking into gear, the same way it had the day I heard the rattlesnake. *Run*, she was telling me. *Get away and don't look back.*

Hamza kept us calm and quiet with almost imperceptible shushes. The leopard stretched, let out a small roar and moved off in the other direction, away into the dark cover of the bush. We all took a deep breath and the engines fired back up. We were safe. The next morning, Hamza said the leopard was probably curious about us. He did not perceive us as a threat – there had been no aggressive body language or posturing. He just stayed, sniffed and watched. It was an easy remark to make in the safety of the camp with the morning sun shooing hungry beasts back into their dens for another night. Whatever the leopard had been thinking, I knew that I had been more scared and in awe than I'd ever been of anything in my life.

Predators are more frightening in the dark. As a diurnal species, active in the day, with comparatively poor nocturnal eyesight, we feel vulnerable at night. But there is something else at play. Over time, and especially within Western cultures, darkness has been presented as something morally bad. It is used as a metaphor for evil, depression, difficulty, hardship and wickedness.

Even those of us who have learned to love the dark aren't exempt. We feel the prickles of hair standing up on the backs of our necks when we hear something rustling in the woods at night. Achluophobia, also known as nyctophobia – fear of the dark – is one of the most common phobias, experienced by around one-third of children, according to the Cleveland Clinic. This number goes down to 3.5 per cent in adulthood, but with light pollution increasing at 10 per cent a year and most of Europe and North America no longer experiencing a naturally dark night, we must ask whether the surveyed adults had ever even experienced true darkness. And if it's true that only a very small percentage of adults are afraid of the dark, then why are we destroying the night at such a rapid pace?

I arrived in Rome on a rainy December evening on a mission to track down that ultimate embodiment of night-time fear: the wolf. I'd told my plans to a colleague from Florence, with whom I worked part-time at a small conservation NGO. I would be hiring a car at Ciampino airport and driving southeast into the mountains of Abruzzo, where wolves were being rewilded. He laughed and called me brave for facing his country's aggressive and impatient drivers, and he wasn't wrong. I was far more worried about Italy's roads than its predators.

When I got behind the wheel, evening was falling in thick fog and rain that settled over the highway, turning the Roman traffic into a blurry line of red tail-lights stop-starting on the A1. Bright oncoming LED headlights streaked across my vision. I sat forward and stiff, not relaxing until I reached the dark embrace of unlit country roads. There, I could see my way again.

Wolves can roam in huge territories, but the mountain town of Pescasseroli, at the centre of Abruzzo National Park, is a popular base for wolf tracking and other mountain activities. My home for the next few days was a small guest room in a nineteenth-century townhouse on its main street.

There I met wildlife guide Andrea De Angelis, who greeted me with an Italian double-cheek kiss and drove us both fifteen minutes out of the village to a muddy field. He wore forest-green corduroy trousers and a frayed wool jumper with a bandana around his head. His movements through the landscape were silent and I felt self-conscious in my loud, rustling synthetic hiking trousers and waterproof jacket.

We walked up a track littered with white granite stones and along a hillside still bright green under low-hanging cloud. I told Andrea that I was trying to understand darkness and fear, which is why I came looking for wolves. He said that he grew up in Rome but studied ecology and moved to the mountains to become a forestry ranger and get away from other people. He said he had been obsessed with wolves since he was a boy.

'The myth is that Rome was founded by the orphans Romulus and Remus, who were raised by a she-wolf,' he said. 'So, as a Roman, maybe I have wolf in my blood.' I pointed to the hillsides, which were covered in sheep droppings, and asked if the wolf population was a problem for the shepherds there.

'In this part of Italy, most people have lived next to wolves for centuries,' he said. 'The people here in Pescasseroli understand that wolves are part of the environment, like the weather. Maybe they lose a few livestock a year to predation. For them, it has not been seen as a big problem.'

We followed a trail into an ancient birch woodland that covered the valley floor between two clusters of hills. The sun dipped behind the soft ridge of mountains in front of us. As we walked, Andrea explained that wolves were never fully eradicated from Italy the way they were in other parts of Europe, Britain and the US. Though hunting and urban development led to the significant decline of wolf populations in Italy from the turn of the twentieth century, legislation by the EU and local government to protect wolves in recent decades, combined with the efforts of organisations like Rewilding Europe, have helped catapult the wolf population back up to healthier numbers. A 2022 national wolf report by the Italian Ministry of Ecological Transition stated that there are more than 3,300 wolves in Italy now. Across Europe, that number is nearing 22,000.

By the time we looped back to the car, night was falling in gentle pinks – a slower sunset at this Mediterranean latitude than its abrupt December descent onto London.

'Tomorrow we must set off early,' Andrea said. 'Wolves are crepuscular, so the best time to see them is right before dawn.' I thought of the Ruaha leopard and the rattlesnake, and wanted to know if wolf tracking would be dangerous, but also didn't want Andrea to think I was a coward.

'Is there anything I need to know? About how to behave around wolves?' I mustered.

'There's no guarantee we'll see them. Let's hope we do. They are amazing animals. Usually, they have been out hunting all night and are full, tired and looking for a good place to rest. I'll pick you up at five a.m.'

My anxiety was not assuaged, and I slept restlessly in the unfamiliar, drafty bedroom.

*

Fear, it turns out, is both learned and inherited. The amygdala is the part of the human brain that controls emotional responses and plays a role in learning and memory. When our bodies are faced with immediate physical danger – let's say the presence of a hungry nocturnal leopard in a nearby bush – these almond-shaped clusters of grey matter prompt fight-or-flight mode to help you physically deal with whatever danger is about to befall you. The amygdala tells the rest of the brain to fire up the adrenal system and release two kinds of stress hormones: cortisol and adrenaline. These in turn activate the body – extra blood rushes to your muscles to prepare you to run and your heart pounds faster to pump that blood out. Your lungs open up so you can take deeper breaths; you get a special shot of blood sugar for energy, and you might start to feel clammy as your blood flow is redirected. Your eyes dilate to help you see in sharper focus and you might get goosebumps – an evolutionary relic from a million years ago, when our ancestors still had thick body hair – and these bumps made the follicles stand up to keep the body alert and warm.

These responses evolved from pure survival instinct. While it's true that now, with all of our technology, human beings are at the top of the food chain, *Homo sapiens* and our smaller primate ancestors lived in trees and caves and were more likely to be hunted than to hunt. In his book *The Wild Life of Our Bodies,* biologist Rob Dunn explains how other species have affected human evolution, and how these early prey responses continue to influence our behaviours today.

He calls our amygdala and adrenals 'a finicky system that can be aroused at the mere idea of a threat' and says that fear might even be our default reaction, calling the fear response a 'bomb in our brain'.

'Now we retaliate against these predators, but for most of our long history of interacting with predators, we did not have guns,' he writes. 'We did not even have the where-withal to pick up and wield sticks. We screamed . . . and ran.' Dunn asserts that, while the brain is doing its best to protect us, it doesn't understand the difference between the threat of a hungry leopard and that of an email from an unhappy manager. It took 6 million years for humans to evolve to our current state. Given that we have only had electric light at night for less than 200 years, our bodies haven't had enough time to evolve out of a fear of the dark.

Nowadays we tend to fear predators among our own species. Wolves haven't been a threat in Europe or North America for at least two centuries, but the fear of rapists and murderers is imprinted on us from childhood, and this fear is particularly acute among women. Often when my research on dark skies comes up in conversation, people baulk. *What about safety? Surely you, as a woman, care more about safety than seeing the stars.* My response is always that it's not dualistic. For starters, there are ways of gently and safely lighting neighbourhoods and cities that are not as wasteful nor as pollutive as the systems we currently have in place, which are ruining habitats and health and causing the disappearance of night. As to the question of safety outside after dark, we must first consider the geophysical fact that darkness is as natural as daytime. Roughly half of our planet is in darkness at any given moment, and darkness is needed for the healthy functioning of almost every natural system on Earth.

There is little data to show a direct correlation between added nighttime lighting and crime reduction. I like to joke that if more light meant more safety, Las Vegas, Nevada would be the safest city on the planet. As with the air we breathe, the experience and enjoyment of darkness without fear of crime or violence should be the right of people of all genders. My friend and colleague Dani Robertson, the Dark Sky Officer for Eryri (Snowdonia) National Park and author of the book *All Through the Night: Why Our Lives Depend on Dark Skies*, put it succinctly: 'Darkness isn't dangerous to women. It's violent men who use the night to aid their crime . . . You could stick a street light on my head and it ain't keeping me safe if a man wants to hurt me.'

Before my wolf trip, I'd started reading Erica Berry's seminal work *Wolfish: The stories we tell about fear, ferocity and freedom*. It is a complex book that weaves together the author's experiences with anxiety, the predatory behaviours of men and Berry's decade of research about a rewilded US wolf known as OR-7, who left his pack in eastern Oregon and wandered hundreds of miles alone in search of a mate. She questions why, in a time and place where wolves present no tangible threat to people's safety, a human would pick up a rifle and kill a wolf in the middle of a forest, and she concludes that humans do not see biological wolves as they are, but rather as symbols and myths that have been constructed from centuries of storytelling and fairy tales.

In this, Berry touches on the crux of our problem with darkness, too. Humans do not understand darkness as a natural ecosystem or habitat. Instead, as with the wolf, we view the dark through generations of storytelling, mythmaking and metaphor. Darkness has become something powerful and scary in our collective psyches, personified by monsters and predators.

At 5 a.m. sharp, Andrea was waiting for me outside the guesthouse. The cobbled street was wet from overnight sleet and shone under orange street lights, which illuminated the Via della Piazza for no one. We got wordlessly into Andrea's car, and he turned the heat on full blast, spewing out stuffy air that smelled of dust and motor oil. I tucked my hands in between my legs and tried to think of what to say as we drove along an empty road through the mountains. It occurred to me that, there in the dark, I was totally at Andrea's mercy. We'd met only the day before. He was driving me on remote roads into the wilderness. He was bigger and stronger than I was. If Andrea wanted to hurt me, he could. I took a deep breath and pushed the idea away.

'So, you are American but live in the UK?' he asked, breaking the heavy silence and my intrusive thoughts. 'I meet a lot of English who come on my tours. I enjoy

English people, but I don't fully understand them.' He hung the statement in a way that suggested there was more underneath it.

'There is a lot left unsaid with the English. I've been there for twelve years and I still sometimes feel like I don't know what's going on,' I replied. 'There is a whole layer to English communication that isn't said out loud.'

He was quiet for a moment, both hands on the wheel, then launched into a story about a situationship (he called it a 'romantic friendship') he had with an English woman that confused him terribly. It seemed like the weight of the morning darkness had created a safe place to open this vulnerable part of himself to a near-stranger. I confided that I, too, had been confused and heartbroken by an Englishman whom I loved deeply and who I knew loved me back but left my life anyway. We sat in our overheated confessional of a car not saying much after that.

It was still dark when Andrea parked on an empty stretch of road along a treeless hill overlooking a farm and ridgeline beyond. It was quiet except for the faraway stirring of cattle somewhere in the unlit valley below.

'This is where I have seen wolves before,' he said, setting up a tripod and switching on a handheld thermal monocular, which he used to scan the hillsides for the white-hot outlines of living creatures on the move in the dark. I pulled on a pair of gloves and looked across the surrounding hills, still only charcoal outlines. Andrea gave me the thermal monocular to have a go, but I spotted nothing. We stood, not talking, until dawn had begun to break, covering the land in a sudden wash of colour.

And then he found something. It was small and four-legged and roaming up the opposite hill about half a kilometre from us. I peered through the monocular and saw the white shape picking its way around boulders and shrubs.

'Has to be a wolf,' Andrea assured me. 'The size and movement are for certain a wolf.' He set to training the bigger tripod telescope on the area while I tracked the wolf's movements up the hill. It came to a halt two-thirds of the way up and there we spotted it through the bigger scope: a mass of grey and rust-red fur, a pointed snout and a bushy tail with that iconic black tuft at the end. The wolf looked so cute and non-threatening there, lying down, having a rest after a hunt.

I thought about Erica Berry's observation that *Little Red Riding Hood* was a tale 'passed on to young girls ... to imbue resilience and strength in a world often inexplicably cruel' and how, in cultures beyond the West, wolves have played positive, heroic and even godlike roles. To some Native American peoples, wolves could be courageous healers 'sent by their creator, a magical spirit often represented as female with an ability to heal and instil courage, to know the night around her as easily as she knows her own bones'. The Cherokee people, for example, believe wolves are watchdogs that hunt on behalf of the spirit Kana'ti. Berry quotes the poem *The Fallen* by Linda Hogan, a member of the Chickasaw Nation, for whom the wolf is immortalised in the stars. The poem tells how the Great Wolf lived in the sky and was the mother of all women, howling their daughters' names. It goes on to admonish those the author calls the 'new people' – white colonisers – for seeing the wolf as the devil and for fearing and killing everything that crossed their path. These wolves, demonised like the darkness they inhabit, died in the name of a deeper fear that white Europeans refused to confront in themselves.

The Italian sun was rising behind me, warming my frozen back, and my eye stayed glued to the lens. My wolf was curled in a rocky outcrop, still but not sleeping. Occasionally, he would stand, circle and reposition, raising his snout and sniffing the air. Andrea said he would be searching for the scent of his pack mates, who were likely roaming around nearby. Although wolves can leave their packs and travel for hundreds of kilometres from their home territory, just as Berry's wolf, OR-7, did in Oregon, they most often live in family groups and stay within a more confined area of a few dozen square kilometres. They hunt, mate, sleep and howl together as a family, not unlike humans.

In New Mexico, where I grew up, wolves were long part of the landscape and, though they were killed off in the mid-twentieth century, they remain an integral part of our state identity. The sports mascot for my alma mater, the University of New Mexico, is the Lobos – the Spanish word for 'wolves'. Attend any UNM sporting event and you'll find crowds of students and alumni chanting *Everyone's a lobo, woof woof woof!* while raising their arm in the air with pointer and pinky fingers up to form the head of a wolf with their hand. The university bookstore is full of merch covered in paw prints and icons of growling grey wolves.

The Lobos are named for Lobo, the King of Currumpaw, a wolf trapped by settler Ernest Thompson Seton in the 1890s. Lobo and his pack were starving because the newly arrived settlers had killed off the elk and bison, and so they'd begun to hunt the settlers' livestock to survive. The ranchers tried to hunt and poison the pack and put a bounty of $1,000 on Lobo's head. Seton set out to capture Lobo but was outwitted by the crafty wolf, who evaded his traps time and again. Seton eventually realised that Lobo's Achilles' heel was his mate, a white wolf known as Blanca. He captured Blanca and used her scent to lure Lobo in, and then killed Blanca in front of him. Seton later wrote a book, *Wild Animals I Have Known*, in which he recounted that he'd heard Lobo howling in grief for two full days afterwards. He said the howls had 'an unmistakable note of sorrow' and were 'no longer the loud, defiant howl, but a long, plaintive wail'. Eventually, Seton captured Lobo, too, but was filled with regret and opted not to behead the wolf. Lobo died of a broken heart the same night.

This experience changed Seton. From that time until he died in 1946, he championed wolves and wrote that it was his wish for people to see that native wild creatures are a precious heritage which people have no right to harm.

Lobo's pelt is kept at the Ernest Thompson Seton Memorial Library and Museum near Cimarron, New Mexico, and the story was made into the 1962 Disney movie *The Legend of Lobo*.

The same week that I travelled to Italy to track Apennine wolves, another New Mexico wolf was causing a stir. A female Mexican grey wolf listed as F2754 was on the move. She had roamed beyond the boundaries put in place as part of the state's wolf-rewilding efforts, a line at Interstate 40 denoting the conservation area. Ecologists had agreed that the Mexican grey wolf's natural habitat seemed to be the Sonoran desert lowlands, while ranchers didn't want wolves prowling freely in the Rocky Mountain meadows where they sent their livestock out for summer grazing. So the boundary was marked on maps at Interstate 40 – an arbitrary line denoting the conservation area, beyond which wild wolves 'shouldn't' go.

It was not the first time the 2-year-old wolf had crossed the line and headed north. The previous year, after she had been collared, she'd gone in the same direction. Her extensive travels had surprised wolf experts and caught the attention of the media. A public competition was held to name her, and seventh-grade student Maesen Whiteside won with the Sanskrit word for 'hope'. F2754 was officially named Asha.

Asha's second foray north of Interstate 40 again captured the public's imagination. Wildlife advocates began using the hashtag #LetAshaRoam alongside photos of the wolf running across the desert in a blur. Was she convinced she'd find her mate in the Sangre de Cristo Mountains? I felt a pang of understanding as I anthropomorphised her along with everyone else. I knew what it was like to feel my destiny in some far-reaching territory, beyond the boundaries of what others said I was allowed to do.

On the day that I met Andrea for our first hike, Asha was identified and captured by the New Mexico Department of Game and Fish. Photos appeared on social media of her lying sedated with a blue mask over her eyes. She would be transferred to a wolf-management facility and paired with a mate and, if successful, released back into the wild after breeding. The news hit me directly in the gut. I sat on the bed in Pescasseroli that morning looking at the photo of Asha lying in the back of a truck, and cried hot, fat tears.

I told Andrea about Asha as we watched our Apennine wolf, free, full and wild. A little while later, he spotted two more wolves trotting down the hills farther away. Likely our wolf's pack mates, he said, who had all been hunting in the area last night. Though I knew that the wolves were all around us, and that if they wanted to they could have surrounded us and attacked, I felt none of the fear I'd experienced with the leopard or the rattlesnake. With his doglike snout that seemed to spread into a goofy grin as he found a better position to rest, I loved this wolf the way I loved Asha, and I said this to Andrea.

'I think I am part wolf,' he returned quietly. 'Something happened to me when I saw my first wolf. I became one of them. I like them better than people. I understand them. They need to roam alone but they are also pack animals. They have the best of everything. I want to find my pack. I roam too much alone.' I could feel the longing and sadness in him, the same way it boiled and froze in me.

The hours of cold began to settle into our bones. It was past 10 a.m. and we were overdue a cappuccino.

The next day, I went to meet with Valerio Reale, the enterprise officer for Rewilding Europe's Apennines branch. Valerio works with artisans and business owners to connect rewilding efforts in Abruzzo National Park with local livelihoods. Rewilding Apennines is headquartered in the nearby town of Pettorano Sul Gizio, a tiny hilltop village bordering the Monte Genzana and Alto Gizio Nature Reserve. It is the type of place you might see on a postcard, with cobbled micro-streets winding in a steep maze to a castle and stone townhouses featuring the fading remains of seventeenth-century murals.

'Rewilding' is a concept that has gained credibility within nature conservation over the past several decades. It has its detractors, who say that attempts to 'reinstate' some natural habitat from the past will always be arbitrary. Early rewilding projects were sometimes criticised for alienating local communities, but Rewilding Europe's organisational principles have come to rely on cultivating buy-in among local stakeholders and then 'letting nature lead'. This means the focus is not on 'restoring' landscapes to an arbitrary past point in time, and there is 'no human-defined optimal point or end state', but rather gentle interventions allow landscapes to regain wildness in their own potentially new ways.

Valerio met me in a draughty office located on the bottom floor of a 300-year-old house and invited me to take a seat.

'Sorry about the mess. Do you eat cheese?' He moved a stack of papers off a desk and pulled half a cheese wheel out of a tiny fridge at the back of the room. I nodded and he pushed the wheel in my direction.

'It's a soft, goat's milk cheese invented by one of the local artisans I work with,' he said, explaining the correlation between a healthy, rewilded landscape and cheese. 'It has to do with the number of vegetal species that are present within fields and mountain meadows, which enrich the diets of the animals. If you don't pasteurise the milk, you're going to keep some of that diversity, some of those microorganisms, in the milk. And that will translate into a more interesting cheese with more flavour. And that will also have a good impact on your intestinal flora.' He told me that wild animals, from wolves to the local griffon vultures, have a role in this process because predators and scavengers contribute significantly to seed dispersal, allowing landscapes to recover and renew plant species naturally.

Valerio and I discussed how the merits of wolf rewilding have been hotly debated, and many people remain staunchly opposed. But he told me research shows time and again that predators are crucial to ecosystems, precisely because they inspire fear. Apex predators like wolves are sometimes called 'keystone species' because they change the behavioural and grazing patterns of their prey, like elk, which in turn affects the growth patterns of shrubs, grasses and trees that the elk browse on. These patterns have a domino effect across the food web, known as a 'cascade'. To take an example: wolves were killed off in Yellowstone National Park in the 1920s, and studies following their successful reintroduction in 1995, more than seventy years later, have shown astonishing ripple effects. The wolves curtailed excess populations of elk, which allowed willow, aspen and cottonwood trees to regrow. The renewed presence of willow stands provided ample, sturdy wood for beaver families and songbirds to repopulate. Beaver dams positively affected spring water runoff and the trees provided needed shade for aquatic populations. The effects went on and on down the cascade. Ecologists call this the 'ecology of fear', and the way that predators affect species and flora distribution are 'landscapes of fear'.

Humans, meantime, create road and vehicle death traps for ground species. We trim lawns and cut down weeds, which otherwise would provide crucial habitats for insect life and small mammals within the overgrowth; we shoot predators because of the fairy tales we were told as children; and we shine bright lights all night, every night – light that travels hundreds of kilometres away from its source in every direction, disorienting birds, ensnaring pollinators, disturbing the mating patterns of aquatic species and scaring off large predators like wolves. If predators cause changes in the ecology of landscapes, then a human-ruled Earth is one giant terra firma of fear that is wildly out of balance.

Now, in Pescasseroli, you can't go anywhere without encountering wolf imagery, wolf merchandise and wolf-themed businesses, many of which are enterprises that Valerio helps connect with the rewilding programme. One night, I ate dinner at a restaurant called La Tana Del Lupo – The Wolf's Den – whose sign featured a cutout image of a black wolf howling against a giant full moon. I had a plate of spaghetti alla chitarra surrounded by posters of majestic grey wolves trotting through deep snow and staring distantly through groves of birch trees. Down the road, in the town of Civitella Alfedena, a café called Il Bar del Lupo sits across the street from the Museum of the Apennine Wolf, where information panels are framed by illustrated wolf prints alongside wolf skeletons and even taxidermised wolf specimens. In Abruzzo, it seems the wolf has not just created a landscape of fear, but an entire new economy.

The morning after Andrea and I spotted the three wolves, we went to a village called Ortona dei Marsi – another hill-top fortress town with tiny winding roads. In the Collegiata di San Giovanni Battista, built in the early 1100s, I thought about the village's medieval residents who had also lived alongside the distant relatives of the wolf families we'd seen. I wondered what they felt about the wolves and tried to imagine what it would have been like walking the streets after dark in the 1300s. Andrea was hungry, and led the way to a small grocery store where a smiling woman handed over squares of pizza cooked that morning. She told Andrea that the previous night the whole town had heard the wolves howling from the hills.

'Probably the same pack we saw,' he said, raising his eyebrows with a knowing smile.

'Can you ask her how it made her feel,' I said. 'Was she afraid?' He translated my question.

'A little afraid, she says. But the wolves are far away. The howling echoes. She says it is a spooky feeling.'

On my final morning in Abruzzo we parked at a picnic area at the base of the Val Fondillo. It was before dawn, and a gentle mist fell through a night that closed around us like velvet curtains. Andrea did not turn on his headlamp, nor did he speak much, just shouldered his backpack and gestured for me to follow him up a slope, past a closed visitor centre. It was completely dark – the night hike I'd been quietly hoping for; a pilgrimage into everything the dark embrace might hold. Sightlessness, uncertainty, predators, wolves, fear.

I didn't know exactly where I was. Andrea was leading us up a set of stairs, across a groomed lawn and onto a rocky trail that needled into the mountains. By now we had spent some time together, but still, intrusive thoughts darted around for a minute. *No one knows where you are, including you. He could be leading you into a trap. It is crazy to follow him into the dark woods.* Echoes of the stories I'd heard over and over. The admonishment for Little Red Riding Hood not to go into the forest. The media headlines in which women are killed for going out after nightfall. The friends' voices: *Aren't you afraid that it's not safe out there in the dark?*

At that moment, I understood that going into the dark would require trust, and that every journey after this would be the same. New lands and connections were not discovered by staying in the comfort of a well-lit room. Safe or not, it was my path to walk into the dark. So I followed Andrea into the lightless woodland, letting my eyes adjust until I could just see the outlines of rocks and shrubs lining the sides of the trail as we climbed. The foliage tightened, and we walked silently in single file. Andrea was surefooted and at ease – he'd probably hiked this path a hundred times in the dark.

After half an hour, the trail opened onto another path, this one wider, leading downhill toward a thin valley to the east. Andrea stopped and surveyed the way, then moved close to me in the shadows.

'This is an old transhumance trail,' he whispered into my ear. 'Shepherds used this road to bring sheep up and down the valley to the coast. This is an ancient place – more than a thousand years old.'

We stayed there for a moment catching our breath. The birds were not yet calling for daybreak. All was silent. And then I heard it – a long, singular wail echoing somewhere far away. A second one joined, and then a third, and my hair stood on end. It was wolves – a choir of howls. They were not close by – probably on the hillside across the valley. The howls continued in a round, as one wolf stopped a moment to breathe and rejoin the choir, alternating back and forth so that they sounded continuously for several full minutes.

I'd heard coyotes calling many times before. Theirs is totally different – a high-pitched, anxious yap. I thought of Lobo's howls of agony for Blanca and how sorrowful they must have been. These howls, though, had no melody of grief. They were the low, primordial song of the pack; a canticle of joy, togetherness and wildness.

Andrea and I stood there at the ancient crossroads long after the dawn chorus ended, perhaps waiting for the right words to say to each other. They never came, so we kept on walking silently as the sun came up.

4

MYTH

Ireland

We couldn't see the river, but we could hear it. I tugged my woollen hat over my ears and squinted into the night. The wind was sharp and bone-cold – new air swept in from the Atlantic Ocean, some distance beyond in the dark. We stood for a moment listening to the sound of rushing water. Low clouds moved overhead like fast grey ships. The dim light of the stars shone through then vanished again. Gradually, the outlines of stone walls appeared: the shadowy ruins of a medieval abbey.

'Does anyone know which direction that is?' asked Georgia, pointing away from the abbey into the night. We shifted, our feet crunching wet gravel. I'm usually good at wayfinding, but the thickness of this particular night had left me disoriented, staring into the sky.

'That's north,' she said. 'And if these clouds cleared off,

we would be able to see Polaris – the North Star – showing the way.'

Georgia MacMillan is the development officer for Mayo Dark Sky Park. Along with her partner, Ged Dowling, she runs Terra Firma Ireland, a social enterprise tour company taking visitors on stargazing trips and eco-tours around County Mayo in the west of Ireland. We were standing near the ruins of Burrishoole Friary, just outside of Newport. A black outline of hills to the north marked the interior of Wild Nephin National Park and the boundary of the dark sky park.

I was here to learn the lesser-known myths of early Celts and pagans – people who had built sacred tombs and stone rows aligned with the sky, like Newgrange and Stonehenge. Led by Georgia and Ged, we would explore Irish myth with a traditional seanchaí, or Irish storyteller. Local residents Jennifer and Celine would join us.

Burrishoole Friary stands on the shore of Clew Bay, a vast inlet that washes the rough Atlantic deep into County Mayo. Zooming out on the map, the bay is shaped a bit like a barking dog or a roaring T-Rex. It divides the county roughly in half from north to south and is filled with hundreds of islets formed of drumlins, which are elongated, teardrop-shaped hills of rock, sand and gravel made by the movement of glaciers. As sea levels rose thousands of years ago, only the tops of these little hills were left exposed. Local legend says there are 365 islets in Clew Bay, one for each day of the year.

Not far from where we were standing on the north coast of the bay, a sixteenth-century pirate queen ruled land and waves from Rockfleet Castle. Grace O'Malley – known as Granuaile, which sounds like 'gron-yuh wail'– learned the art of seafaring from her father. She inherited his position as leader of their clan and a vast territory of western Ireland and its coast, marrying twice, travelling huge distances by ship, and purportedly giving birth to a son at sea an hour before fending off attackers. Her life has been embellished with legends, but she was undoubtedly fierce and formidable. Records show that she travelled to London in 1593 to meet with Queen Elizabeth I, successfully petitioning for her family's release from prison. Legend has it that Grace refused to bow to Elizabeth during the meeting.

Above us the sky cleared for a moment, and Georgia pointed out a constellation.

'You can see Cassiopeia,' she said, using a green laser pointer to trace a group of stars shaped like the letter M. 'Sometimes we call Cassiopeia "Granuaile" because it is one of the circumpolar constellations, which go around the North Star like a clock face every night. And Granuaile navigated her way by the North Star in the old days. You can see it's shaped like an M – for Mayo, as we like to say here!' She laughed.

Polaris is nicknamed the 'North Star' because it appears to sit directly above the North Pole. Because of this, the star also seems not to move through our night sky, as Earth effectively spins 'underneath' it. From the Northern

Hemisphere, you can find due north by drawing a line from Polaris down to the horizon.

'Rockfleet Castle is just a few miles up the road, and Granuaile and her clan likely used this friary as a trading post and supply centre,' Georgia said, circling the North Star with the laser. 'Granuaile was an immensely knowledgeable navigator and would have used the North Star here to navigate her ships around this whole coastline.'

Led by Granuaile, the O'Malley clan wielded significant power over the region, which at that time was well-trafficked by traders and pirates from around the Anglo-Celtic archipelago and further afield in Europe and North Africa. The clan tolled incoming ships, using their extensive knowledge of the complex geography of the Irish coast to maintain control of its meandering shorelines and countless islands.

We left the abbey and drove up a curving road the width of a single vehicle, lined on both sides by unforgiving hedges. Rain fell in fits and starts, hitting the roof of the van in a metallic clatter. It was not yet 9 p.m., but we were nearing the winter solstice and it had been fully dark for hours.

'This is the type of place you'd see a banshee,' Jennifer said, and we all laughed uneasily.

I first heard about banshees on a solo trip around Ireland in my early twenties, hopping from hostel dorms to pubs for Guinness and traditional music sessions. While staying at a bunkhouse in a remote part of County Galway, I took a walk one night with a handsome scuba diver from

Dublin named Aidan. We went up an unpaved track away from the roaring fire in the hostel's common room, which overlooked Ireland's only fjord. Near the top of the hill, we stopped, and Aidan eyed the mist around us, popping the collar of his peacoat up around his neck. It was winter and the wind was moving the fog around like ghosts.

'God, I hope we don't see any banshees,' he said with a little grin. 'Do you know about them?'

I shook my head. It was a word I'd only heard in passing – the Irish legend of a spectral woman dressed in white.

'They used to tell us stories . . . freaked me out as a kid,' he said. 'Banshees are like women of the hills. Like this mad ghost woman dressed all in white who comes out at night. And she can tell the name of who will die.'

I learned that long ago in Ireland there were women who sang laments at funerals, and that people said they could hear the singing – their keening – even before someone died. Over time, the idea of the banshee evolved – she was said to appear only at night and only for a handful of the most important families as a predictor of death. She morphed into a scary figure and her tearful keening was corrupted into an eerie screeching so shrill that it could break glass windows. Now, the banshee is often depicted with her white hair matted, eyes red, hands curled into claws, and mouth open in a vampiric growl. Sometimes she is skeletal, decrepit, demonic. Sometimes with a pointed, snakelike tongue or wilted face.

But the banshee is also present in some of the oldest Celtic stories. The word itself comes from the Old Irish ben síde, meaning 'woman of the fairy mound'. In Irish myth, the fairy people are known as the Aos Sí, descendants of a race of gods called the Tuatha Dé Danann. These stunningly beautiful, human-sized creatures were said to have supernatural powers and used the tumuli – burial mounds dotted all over Ireland – as portals into the human realm.

Among the most evocative depictions of the Aos Sí is the 1911 painting *The Riders of the Sidhe* by Scottish artist John Duncan. A work of Celtic Revival painted in rich blue, red, green and gold, the image shows a group of fairy folk parading through a forest, sitting tall astride white horses. With flowing garments and saddle blankets and long, golden hair, they are not dissimilar in appearance to Tolkien's elf race. In the painting, each carries a magical talisman: the tree of life, love grail, sword and crystal stone. The scene is set on Bealtaine, the pagan May festival halfway between the spring equinox and the summer solstice.

At a dead end, Ged parked the van in front of a bothy. The small stone cabin had two square windows that glowed amber on either side of its wooden door. These were the only sources of light for miles, and very inviting in the freezing wind and rain.

Inside, silver candelabras held long, flickering candles dripping with red wax. A tall, white-haired man stood behind a table covered in a red cloth, the candles casting his super-sized shadow into one corner. He wore a navy blazer over a brown woollen jumper and smiled as we blustered in the door, dripping and windswept. He introduced himself as Dan O'Donoghue, a traditional storyteller who 'does a bit of magic' and 'spent some time in Las Vegas'.

The seanchaí, or Gaelic storytellers, were historically both entertainers and record-keepers, orally passing down important information, including laws, literature and family lineages, while also keeping chieftains, kings and families company around the hearth during long winter evenings. Traditional storytelling is still alive in Ireland and the wider Gaelic world, where it is an art form and academic pursuit on par with poetry, music and visual art. It is not unusual to find storytelling on the bill during an open mic night or traditional music session, particularly in the west of Ireland.

We sat down at a row of folding chairs before the red table and Georgia produced a flask of hot cocoa. After performing some card tricks and sleight of hand, Dan settled into a story.

'In Homer's *Iliad*, there's a character mentioned called Orion the Hunter, whom the stars have painted in the sky,' he said, his voice rising and falling with a song-like rhythm. 'Now, the constellation Orion is up there standing proud aside his favourite hound, Sirius, the Dog Star. But here in Mayo, we don't call them that. We call him Daithí Bán, the bog monster. And as for the faithful hound, he is actually Daithí Bán's deadly and sworn enemy, the Dobhar Chu.'

Dan proceeded to tell the story of Daithí Bán being

pursued by the Dobhar Chu, his voice undulating like soft hills. The story was a mix of Homer's *Iliad*, Mayo myth and Dan's own interpretation, sprinkled with the occasional rhyme or joke. We clutched our mugs of cocoa and listened like kids as shadows flickered off the stone walls. The rain and mountains and darkness outside felt like a cosy blanket around us, kept safe there in the warmth of the bothy, surrounded by good company.

Dan's story ended with the love interest – goddess Diana – setting Daithí Bán and the Dobhar Chu, both deceased by the end, into the stars. 'Which means that to this very day,' said Dan with a mischievous grin, 'you can go out under the night sky – well, not this particular night sky ...' he chuckled. 'You can go out there and you can see Daithí Bán and the Dobhar Chu. Or you see Orion and Sirius. Who knows, who cares? All that matters is that the stars have written their stories in the sky. And they are there for you and for me to tell their stories for evermore. Mad, truly mad.'

In her book on pagan Ireland, *Old Ways, Old Secrets*, Jo Kerrigan writes that Ireland's ancient tales were meant to be told by human voices, as a collective experience, rather than read from pages in a book. This storytelling took place in the evenings, as families and clans gathered around a hearth on long winter nights.

'[Stories] were an experience in which everyone shared – whether they laughed, wept or mourned,' writes Kerrigan.

'A well-told story might go on all night, with digressions added, depending on comments from the crowd.'

One of my favourite essays on darkness is a 2009 *Guardian* article by Jeanette Winterson. 'I have noticed that when all the lights are on, people tend to talk about what they are doing – their outer lives,' she writes. 'Sitting round in candlelight or firelight, people start to talk about how they are feeling – their inner lives. They speak subjectively, they argue less, there are longer pauses.'

She goes on to suggest that we are more creative in darkness, an idea backed up by studies in psychology. A 2013 study from two German universities described how 114 undergraduate students were seated in a small room with a light hanging directly above their desks. Illumination levels varied, with some under dim light at only 150 lux, some under medium light at 500 lux and some under very bright light at 1,500 lux. Participants were given a few minutes to acclimate and then asked to find the optimal solution to a series of creative insight problems, and to self-rate how free from constraints they felt. Those in the dimly lit room solved significantly more problems correctly than those in the brightly lit room, and felt freer and less inhibited than their brightly illuminated counterparts.

The researchers concluded that darkness elicits a feeling of being free from constraints and also triggers a risk-taking, explorative processing style. This may well be why so many of us get our best ideas at night, love listening to music in the evenings and tell the best stories around a campfire.

Early Celtic and pagan people watched the stars closely and their culture was deeply connected to the patterns they found in nature. The word for weather in Irish – aimsir – is the same word that is often used for time and also for grammatical tenses, the expression of past, present and future. The veil to the land of the Aos Sí was said to be thin at dusk and dawn, so you were more likely to encounter fairies around those times of day, and at festivals like Yule, Midsummer, Samhain and Bealtaine, which mark the transitions between seasons.

The early Irish calendar, known as the Coligny Calendar, begins its year at Samhain, on 31 October, when the northern world is beginning its darkest phase.

Many early Celtic sites, such as portal tombs like the one at Newgrange in County Meath, are aligned with the solstices and equinoxes. On the winter solstice, the light of the dawn sunrise perfectly aligns with the Newgrange tomb's corridor, illuminating the passageway and lighting up a spiral motif at the back of the chamber. The passage is a portal linking two worlds, such that when sunlight hits the spiral, it opens a vortex that lets the dead complete their journey from this world to the Otherworld, the land of the fairies.

Over time, people have created myths, legends and stories to explain or warn about things we experience under the cover of night, and to pass that information along in a memorable way. *Little Red Riding Hood* may have started as a warning for children to keep safe from predators, but, over time, it ended up profoundly villainising the wolf. Could the same be said of the banshee or, more broadly, the dark?

The banshee's original role was not necessarily as a harbinger of death. In his book *Mayo Folk Tales*, local historian and storyteller Tony Locke wrote that she was a 'protector or guardian-angel-type spirit' originating from the ancient Celtic goddess, the Morrigan. She was mentioned in a collection of Irish myths called the Ulster Cycle, was associated with war, destiny and fertility, and could foretell the deaths of soldiers in battle. Locke said that the belief in banshees may well have come from 'the Church's dislike of the Irish tradition of women singing a lament to mourn the passing of a family member', and that to discourage this practice, 'the keeners were turned into banshees'. A 2022 NPR radio show, *Celtic Cultural Minute*, likewise suggested that the Catholic Church discouraged keening, regarding it as a pagan practice, and the influential role of the keening women in their communities was likely seen as a threat.

In pre-Christian mythology, the feminine or female was closely associated with darkness and winter. Among the most important figures in Irish mythology is the Cailleach Béara or the Hag of Béara, a seasonal deity-spirit ruling the winter months between Samhain on 31 October and Bealtaine on 1 May. Her name translates as 'veiled one', hinting at her connection to the darker season. The word

'Cailleach' is related to words for old woman, witch, sorceress, wise woman, fortune-teller and bone mother. She is the archetypal wise crone ushering in the harsh colder months, associated with the creation of the land, and is a patron of wolves and deer; in short, she is the 'great mother'. Some tales describe the Cailleach as turning to stone on Bealtaine in May and reverting to life on Samhain in October – the start of the Celtic year – in time to rule over the dark months.

On the Scottish folklore blog, Wee White Hoose, writer and artist Fee Cuimeanach, says the Cailleach was not a destructive or evil deity but rather a transformative force: 'Without her necessary culling of new growth in winter, no life would survive the harsh weather through to the following spring . . . She is the keeper of the seed; the guardian of the essential life force.'

Many traditions around the world have a similar feminine figure connected to darkness. Often these are associated with transformation, fertility and the cycle of death and re-birth. These are usually feared not so much because they are scary but because they represent concepts of the unknown: change, death or the shadow self.

In Greek myth, Nyx was the goddess of night – a primordial deity born from Chaos at the beginning of time. Together with Erebus, the god of night, she gave birth to Light and Day, Sleep, Death, Strife, Pain and the Fates. She was believed to have the power to impact humans in good and bad ways, and to bring sleep and rest or death. Nyx was older and stronger than Zeus, and the only goddess he ever feared. However, Nyx was never referred to as evil nor worshipped by any cults; rather, her role was foundational in the cyclical nature of time and the natural order of the world. As darkness, she was so crucial and ancient that she existed almost before and outside the pantheon.

Nyx's Hindu equivalent is the Vedic goddess Ratri, a powerful maternal figure that bestows life strength. She represents the cyclic patterns of the cosmos. Ratri is described as a benign deity who offers rest and renewed vigour and who may be invoked to ensure safety through the hours of darkness. She is characterised as a protector of livestock, indicating that her original purpose was protection from predators that might attack a farmer's cattle and horses at night. The Cailleach's earliest stories were also about guiding and protecting people and livestock through long, harsh Celtic winters.

In Mexico, the striking Aztec death goddess Ītzpāpālōtl was known as the queen of the Tzitzimimeh 'star demons'. The Tzitzimimeh had a double role in Aztec religion: they were protectresses of the feminine and progenitresses of humankind. The Tzitzimimeh were also associated with the stars, especially the stars that can be seen around the Sun during a solar eclipse. After the introduction of Christianity to Mexico, this was interpreted as the Tzitzimimeh attacking the Sun, thus creating the belief that during a solar eclipse, the Tzitzimimeh would descend to Earth and possess men – another 'dark feminine' threat to a patriarchal system.

The vilification of pagan beliefs, which centred women as powerful wisdom-holders, gatekeepers of the spiritual realms and the providers of life out of darkness, continued throughout the Christianisation of the Western world. From the fifteenth to the eighteenth centuries, women would be condemned to death as witches because they practised ancient, nature-based healing traditions that competed with the Christian god and the Church's influence. Druids, who were the keepers of ancestral weather and sky knowledge, were stripped of their priestly functions when Christianity took over Britain and Ireland. Celebrations of natural seasons were changed – Yule was turned into the date for the birth of Jesus; Ostara, celebrated on the spring equinox, when days and nights are roughly even in length, was made into the date of Jesus's death at Easter.

And so it was with *Little Red Riding Hood* and later fairy tales about the dangers of darkness. These stories originally had an instructive purpose, either to explain some natural phenomenon or to instil survival skills. Over time and increasingly through religious lenses, the darkness in these stories took on sinister and evil aspects. As they transformed into moralistic tales, darkness became a bad place to which the Judeo-Christian god was opposed. The Bible is filled with the language of light and dark; for example, 1 John 1:5 states that 'God is light, and in him is no darkness at all.' In describing him this way, John was asserting the Christian god's absolute moral purity and omniscience. Light in the Christian view was equal to knowledge and purity, while darkness represented immorality and evil. Satan – the Christian god's opponent – was, of course, labelled the 'prince of darkness'.

To learn more about Celtic ancestral connections to the stars, Georgia and Ged suggested I visit several archeoastronomy sites, where structures were purposely lined up with the movements of the Sun, Moon and stars. The first was Killadangan, a stone row near Croagh Patrick, the most sacred mountain in Ireland. 'If you go there at sunset on the winter solstice, the standing stones line up perfectly with the sun setting into a niche in Croagh Patrick,' Ged told me.

The stones sit unassumingly on a patch of salt marsh along the southern shore of Clew Bay. The only evidence of the stone row was a brown sign pointing to the site as a stop on the Clew Bay Archaeological Trail. I trod carefully towards the water, the bog squishing like a soaked sponge under my feet, picking through high tufts of salt marsh grass. Finally, the row appeared – four boulders lined up from shortest to tallest, pointing southwest towards a dip in the towering peak of Croagh Patrick. There were two more stones a few metres away, which archaeologists think may have formed part of a stone circle and cooking area, making this a significant Druid ceremonial site.

A strong sea wind pushed against my back and filled my lungs with sharp air. Cars whooshed by on the road, their drivers uncaring or unaware of the ancient site just beyond their windscreens. I tried to imagine the sun setting in a ball of fire behind Croagh Patrick and thought about how the Neolithic people who celebrated here had felt the same cold wind whipping against their faces as they held their ceremonies on the winter solstice. How would they have felt watching our sun slink low through the dip in the mountainside and then the stars rise over the bay?

The night sky that people saw several millennia ago would have been a little different to ours. This is because of a phenomenon known as precession, in which the Earth is slightly 'wobbling' on its axis, a bit like a spinning top that sways as it spins. Due to precession, Earth would have been at a slightly different angle 6,000 years ago, when Neolithic sites were constructed in Ireland. Modern astronomers can model this using software that shows us what the sky would have looked like at any era in history.

Archaeologists have speculated for decades about the sky connections in the rock carvings of the Neolithic cairns across Ireland. The art at Newgrange is considered among the most sophisticated of its time in the world, and scientists have said that some of the carvings at its sister tomb, Knowth, might be lunar maps depicting a naked-eye view of the Moon's dark patches; these are called mare, meaning 'sea' in Latin. In County Meath at Cairn T, on Sliabh Na Calliagh, which is named for the winter goddess, the rays of the equinox sunrise shine down the passageway and illuminate an inner chamber filled with carvings. These are thought to be a star map or astral guide of some kind. The Druids' choice to associate that equinox cairn with the Cailleach seems deliberate – a way of tracking the end and beginning of the long, dark winter.

After Killadangan, I drove a few miles up the road to see another important Neolithic site: the Boheh Stone. It lay hidden behind an abandoned house overgrown with ivy: a rock outcropping topped by several slabs of stone covered in the same spiral motifs that were carved at Newgrange. I noted the cup and ring marks consisting of a small depression surrounded by concentric circles, as well as keyhole motifs and numerous spirals. Estimates say there are some 250 carvings on the Boheh Stone, dating from as early as 3800 BCE.

Historian Gerry Bracken uncovered the stone in 1981. Through a series of observations from the site, he discovered that on two dates a year –18 April and 24 August – the setting sun from that angle appears to roll like a ball down the slope of Croagh Patrick, a phenomenon the Neolithic artists who carved the stone were surely aware of. Bracken later wrote that he believed the dates, together with the equinoxes and solstices, broke the prehistoric year into three equal parts, with the period from April to August forming the food-growing period for Neolithic farmers.

More recently, in 2023, historian Rónán Lynch published a book in which he claimed to have discovered the meaning of the Boheh Stone's carvings when viewed with two other nearby stones. Using astronomy software, his team mapped the night sky over County Mayo in 4200 BCE. They found that, due to Earth's precession wobble, the Southern Cross – a constellation now only visible from the Southern Hemisphere – would have been visible, slung very low along the Irish horizon, until around 4100 BCE.

'Our ancestors understood and mapped out complex astronomical concepts such as the precession of the equinoxes, which is a cycle of almost 26,000 years,' he said, claiming his findings disprove earlier theories that the cross-like markings found on the stones were later Christian additions.

In *Island of the Setting Sun*, authors Anthony Murphy and Richard Moore suggested there is evidence that Ireland's megalithic sites were laid out along sacred terrestrial lines that formed a grid of intersecting pathways with a complex sky–ground arrangement. Many of the rows or arrangements of sites line up with specific celestial events. They connected these sites with sky events through place names, myths and legendary figures. The solstice and equinox lines are easiest to trace – objects are built along them to line up with the setting sun on those days. Others form alignments with the rising of the star Sirius or the Moon.

In some cases, these lines seem to link multiple sites across vast stretches of Ireland, some many miles from each other. Murphy and Moore call this the 'cosmic grid'. Megalithic people saw landscape features on the horizon as natural aids in their astronomical studies, often naming these features for whatever astronomical event occurred in that direction.

Anthony Murphy wrote in a subsequent article that one such astronomical line links the mouth of the Boyne River in the east with the Hill of Slane, where Saint Patrick lit his famed 'Easter' fire, and on to the summit of Croagh Patrick in the west.

'It connects some of the most significant places associated with Ireland's national saint, and at the same time reflects an ancient cosmology, which predates Saint Patrick by three and a half millennia. There seems no limit to what the ancients were capable of,' he wrote.

It would seem that Saint Patrick indeed visited the sites that were of great importance to the people he met when he arrived in the 400s CE. Eventually, he assigned Christian meanings to these places to convert the Irish to Christianity. The mountain Croagh Patrick was an ancient pagan site long before Patrick climbed it and, at its top, supposedly banished the snakes from Ireland. The Boheh Stone and Killadangan stone row are two such proofs of Croagh Patrick as a place of much earlier pagan worship. Likewise, prehistoric cairns and an earthen fort have been discovered near the mountain's summit.

Croagh Patrick was also the site of a festival for the god Lugh, who, along with the Cailleach, was among the pantheon of the early Tuatha Dé Danann fairy folk. In a 2016 *Irish Times* article, Patrick Claffey wrote that Croagh Patrick was 'the kind of place where "hierophonies" might happen', defining hierophonies as 'moments of meeting between the sacred and the profane, heaven and earth, which our ancestors, with their openness to divine interventions of all kinds, saw as miraculous encounters with the divine Other'.

Across the valley, I could see the pathway that walkers follow when they make their annual religious pilgrimage up the mountain in late July. Until 1976, it was common for Christian pilgrims to ascend Croagh Patrick after sunset, making the five-hour return trek after nightfall. The church authorities eventually outlawed nighttime ascents, supposedly because too many people were using it as an all-night drinking session.

Irish journalist Tom Gillespie performed the pilgrimage six times, five of which were at night. He wrote in the *Connaught Telegraph* in 2023, 'One of the advantages of climbing in the dark, with a bad bicycle lamp, was you had no idea of how far away or close it was to the summit. You had to rely on ascending [sic] pilgrims as to the distance. But all delivered the same encouraging answer when questioned: "It's just around the next corner."'

I drove down from the Boheh Stone, back out along the main road and pulled into Croagh Patrick's car park. As it was deep winter, there were few people around and the cafés were closed, so I wandered up to the trailhead and looked at the mountain. From there, it seemed enormous. At 764m (2,507 feet), it is Ireland's fourth tallest mountain and its conelike shape made the trail appear steep and treacherous. I thought about Tom Gillespie's words. Maybe the night was once full of things to fear and warn against. But making such a journey in the dark could also save you the anxiety of knowing how tough the coming path was and how far was left to climb. The pilgrimage was an act of trust.

On my final night in Ireland, I took a walk alone in Mayo Dark Sky Park. Now, after experiencing nighttime in a few different places, I'd begun to notice that there were various kinds of darkness. Sometimes it was featherlight, spacious, starry, almost infinite; other times it wrapped around me like a quilt, thick with mist or fog. This particular night was fuzzy and dizzying. A thin layer of cloud put a soft filter over Jupiter hanging big and bright, its edges blurry above the mountaintops.

I stood on the path and listened. Everything was quiet, the air muted across an expanse of bogland that stretched out for several miles, ending in a row of low mountains. My eyes hadn't yet adjusted to the darkness, and I strained to find evidence of the path. For a moment, I saw a tangle of weird light moving in front of me – a strange shape floating like fog. It was probably my eyes playing tricks. Or was it? I began to feel a bit freaked out and exposed, standing alone in the middle of the bog, and couldn't help but think of wild-eyed banshees with matted hair and claws for fingers. What unsettled me most was that there was simply nothing out there. No roads, houses or even walking trails. Impenetrable, unknown and dark.

A sixth of Ireland's landmass is covered in peat bog, which is 8 per cent of the total blanket bog in the entire world. Bogs are formed when undecomposed plant material forms a thick layer of peat soil that gets deeper over hundreds of thousands of years. The surface is covered in moss and the soil stays spongy. Sometimes the peat thickens into a rich, dark mud that was, for centuries, cut into blocks and burned for winter fuel; though this practice is slowly being phased out as the importance of peatland for biodiversity and carbon storage has been recognised. But farming peat for fuel has been an important livelihood in Ireland for hundreds of years. Other times, a layer of moss forms over the bogland, concealing unknown depths that can be treacherous to walk over. Peat bogs also notoriously generate their own weather systems, producing unexpected fogs that can be disorienting and dangerous.

A rich mythology has grown around boglands, both in Ireland and around the world. I thought the strange light I saw might have been will-o'-the-wisp, or atmospheric ghost lights, which are common around bogs and marshes at night. These hovering glimmers or balls of light have been attributed to malicious spirits or fairies intent on leading weary travellers into treacherous parts of the bog. The Irish relate this legend to the jack-o'-lantern carved at Halloween, in which a drunk man named Jack or Will does a deal with the devil to pay his bar tab and ends up forced to wander Earth as a lost soul carrying a carved turnip with a candle inside.

Some incidents of will-o'-the-wisp can be explained as a combination of methane and phosphine, which can self-ignite to form swamp gas lights. But the sheer number of similar lights seen in a variety of terrains around the world, not all of them marshland, still makes for compelling folklore. These stories include the Hessdalen lights, unidentified lights seen over a few miles of a rural valley in central Norway; the Naga fireballs, glowing lights said to rise out of the Mekong River in Thailand; and the Marfa ghost lights, often spotted hovering above the horizon outside a small desert town in southwest Texas. What I find most interesting about these stories is that, in them, it isn't darkness that's scary but the lights.

It is the unknown we fear. And the human mind has a propensity to describe – sometimes at great length and complexity – things we experience but don't understand.

Eventually, I began to make out the Pleiades – my favourite cluster of stars whose name I'd learned in New Zealand as Matariki, the sign of the Māori new year. These were the same stars that the Diné people of the southwest US called the Sparkling Seeds, which give instructions for the corn-planting season. Like Jupiter, the stars were fuzzy from the thin layer of cloud. The moment of fear passed. Looking at the familiar sky, I felt safe again – the stars were a constant and the heavens had always been there.

I kept walking, taking one teeny footstep in front of the other. It was hard to see if the terrain was going up or down, or if there were obstacles – it felt like each step was reaching into the void. I thought of the pilgrims who ascended Croagh Patrick in the dark, trusting they'd make it to the top and taking blind encouragement from other walkers. *You're almost there. Not much further now.*

In learning about the myths of the dark, it seemed I had in some ways demystified it. When I reframed those scary stories and set them back into their original context, they became real and relatable. The banshees were not terrifying, evil harbingers of death – they were women like me. Grieving women with beautiful voices who sang mournful songs to ease the agony of loss. The English word 'keen' comes from the Irish word caoin – to cry or weep. The act of keening had been a ritual of huge importance to help the deceased soul move on. It was practised by experienced women elders who were responsible for carrying and expressing a whole community's grief. The keener's cries or wails of sorrow were often described as eerie or etheric – raw sounds brought up from the depths of the body.

It made me profoundly sad to consider how keeners had been villainised and how much of Ireland's rich tradition of collective musical mourning had been wiped out. In much of the Western world, even the act of crying now has a strong stigma attached to it. People who dare to express grief or pain in public are labelled as unhinged, overdramatic or crazy. Yet tears are a natural physical expression of strong emotion. Imagine if society dictated that we hold in the other types of liquids that regularly need to come out. We would be very sick indeed.

As I drove back to my hotel later, I listened to recordings taken in 1955 of keeners from the west of Ireland. The voices were comforting in a mesmeric, almost trance-like way. The high, etheric soprano that Irish women are so well known for reminded me of the rhythmic songs of Diné singers performing Indigenous ceremonies or, at moments, even the guttural vibrations of Mongolian throat singers.

For millennia, the sky, stars, Moon and land were inter-twined with people's ways of life. Priests were also weather forecasters; pirates were astronomers; gardeners were heal-ers; singers were therapists. The Tuatha Dé Danann were a supernatural race of fairy gods who physically interacted with our world through seasons and natural cycles. Myth and legend were real until Christianity rewrote the story. And the night sky held the keys to finding our way, both physically and spiritually.

With this understanding of what once connected us, and also what separated us from the sky, I wanted to learn more about astronomy: how it developed over time and evolved from myth into hard science. And for that, I would journey to the centre of the world.

5

EARLY ASTRONOMY

Uzbekistan

On a cold winter night, a man stands on a hill above a wide plain in the Central Asia desert. His blue robes, embroidered with golden flowers befitting a king, sway in the icy wind. A waxing moon casts a silver glow onto his headdress – a silken chalma that wraps neatly around his head and knots at the front. Before him, a maze of streets spreads into the dark. At this late hour, the great capital of Transoxiana – Samarkand – is asleep.

The man lifts a flat, metal astrolabe and aims it at a star on the eastern horizon. He peers through a tiny eyepiece, then spins the plates until they rest in place and makes a note in a book illuminated by a flickering oil lamp. In a matter of months, on this very hill, construction would begin on the largest astronomical observatory in the world.

The year is 1420, and the man is Ulugh Beg – the favoured grandson of Uzbek leader Amir Timur, or Tamerlane.

Ulugh Beg was only twenty-six when he established his grand observatory at Samarkand. It would become one of the most influential astronomical observatories of the medieval world, supported by scientific study conducted at his madrasa, built a few years earlier in the centre of Samarkand's main square, the Registan. Ulugh Beg would eventually take the helm of the Timurid Empire, ruling from Samarkand, a jewel among Silk Road cities and one of the most cosmopolitan trade centres of that time. But his first and true passion remained science, and he spent much of his adult life looking up at the night sky from the hillside observatory.

Six centuries later, I stood on the same hill on a spring morning. I'd come to the Ulugh Beg Observatory Museum to learn more about the medieval astronomer's life and the wider story of Persian astronomy.

Curator Saodat Yusupova greeted me at the entrance to the museum and, as we walked, she outlined Ulugh Beg's life story from the time he became the regent of Transoxiana at age fifteen until his assassination by his own son in 1449.

'From a young age, Ulugh Beg showed his skills in mathematics and astronomy,' she explained. 'He was interested in the stars. That's why his grandfather, the emperor Timur, invited the best teachers for him.' She pointed to a mural of Ulugh Beg in the museum's entryway. He stood enrobed in

gold, holding a book, surrounded by white-bearded profes-
sors with astronomical instruments including an astrolabe
and a celestial globe. Behind him, stars twinkled in a dark
sky decorated with constellations and a zodiac wheel embellished with twirling Islamic motifs.

The observatory was built at the highest point in
Samarkand, above the Sieb River. On a satellite map, you
can see that it is oriented with absolute precision along a
north–south line. When it was built, the entire structure
was surrounded by a three-storey building covered in the
blue mosaics for which the Timurid Empire became famous.
However, after Ulugh Beg's assassination, the above-ground
structures were razed and the observatory's precise location
was lost for centuries. Finally, in 1908, a Russian archae-
ologist named Vassily Vyatkin found the buried ruins after
years of searching.

At first glance, there is not much to see of Ulugh Beg's
historical observatory now, so little remains of what was
effectively the biggest and busiest astronomical institution
of the medieval world. The site is almost empty apart from
a small museum built in the 1970s, and the mosaic-covered
iwan, or entrance portal, that opens into a preserved underground section. The footprint of the former structure is now
outlined in brick around the underground portion, giving a
good indication of its former size, which would have been
about that of an average Ferris wheel lying on its side, with
a cylindrical structure rising around it.

I stepped out of the April sun, which was already hot

despite the early hour, and peered into a dark shaft containing the underground remains of a giant quadrant – a curved device used to take angular altitude measurements for astronomy and navigation. The telescope was not invented for another 200 years after Ulugh Beg; it was first used by Galileo to observe the night sky in 1610. So this quadrant was Ulugh Beg's primary way of observing celestial objects.

Saodat explained that, typically, quadrants were small, handheld instruments that could be used for navigation. But Ulugh Beg's was huge – a massive arch used to chart the progress of the Sun, Moon and stars across the sky. The arch would have been 63 metres long, curving partway underground and then jutting up into the air in a large quarter circle. A trench was hewn into the hillside to minimise turbulence. Light from a celestial body would pour in through a controlled opening in the roof and fall at a point on the arch depending on the height of the object in the sky. A trackway along the arch was marked very precisely with degrees and minutes.

We peered down into the trench together and Saodat pointed out the treacherous-looking, narrow stone stairways on either side of the trackway.

'Stairs and doors on different levels gave the astronomers access to the arch so they could make a note of where the light fell. With this, they could accurately chart the positions of stars, the length of the year, the local time and the angle of the Earth's tilt,' she explained. 'Timekeeping was an important part of astronomy back then because people didn't yet have a clear grasp of what years, days and hours really were.'

Ulugh Beg was a reluctant ruler. His first love was science, and although he was trained in the military arts, he was not interested in political jostling. The people around him – his spiritual advisors and his family – used that to their advantage. Everything I learned about Ulugh Beg suggested to me he was a sensitive soul, both spiritual and highly cerebral. Saodat said that he even predicted the date of his own death using the stars.

During the Middle Ages, the lines between science and religion were blurry. Astrology – the study of how the planets and stars were believed to affect humans or predict the future – was widely used. Muslim rulers found the stars useful for following religious rituals, including daily prayers and fasting periods at set times, setting the direction to Mecca and making predictions. The scientific study of the stars was funded largely to enable political and religious pursuits. Ulugh Beg was notable for the rigorous methodology and precision with which he compiled his star catalogue. Some scholars even suggest it was a precursor to the modern scientific method.

A few days before, I'd met with Shuhrat Ehgamberdiev, the director of the Ulugh Beg Astronomical Institute. Part of the Uzbek Academy of Sciences, it is the oldest scientific institution in the whole of Central Asia, and it runs all of the major astronomical observatories in Uzbekistan, including the region's largest telescope on Mount Maidanak.

We sat in a cavernous boardroom at the institute's office in Tashkent, the modern capital city of Uzbekistan, surrounded by cases of historical telescopes and wooden clocks.

'This is a copy of a page from one of Ulugh Beg's original star catalogue manuscripts that is in the library in Paris,' said Shuhrat, showing me a framed illustration of the constellation Cepheus portrayed as a bearded man in blue robes. 'But we think that this is actually a portrait; this is the real image of Ulugh Beg. When you go to Samarkand, you will see a modern statue that portrays Ulugh Beg like Timur – a big warrior with muscles. But Ulugh Beg was not like that. Ulugh Beg was a scientist. He was a nerd like us,' he laughed.

At the historical observatory, I stood facing south towards the portal. It was still early, and the Sun was only partway up to my left. Thanks to Ulugh Beg's precision in aligning the quadrant with the north–south meridian, it was easy to tell the approximate time of day. When the Sun lined up with the quadrant, it would be noon.

I thought about all of the astronomers and stargazers who had looked up at the night sky throughout human history. Several thousand years had passed between the time of the Neolithic people, whose solstice-aligned stone rows I'd seen in Ireland, and Ulugh Beg. In the intervening centuries, the Ancestral Puebloans had built their great cities in what is now New Mexico and Colorado around 1500 BCE, tracking the Sun's movements and etching comets and other celestial events on their walls.

On the other side of the world, in China, ancient astronomers had recorded eclipses and calendars onto oracle
bones. The Babylonians had created elaborate star catalogues as early as 1000 BCE and were the first to divide the
night sky into shapes and constellations. Early Greek astronomers, including Aristotle and Hipparchus, had tracked the
movements of the sky and theorised that Earth was at the
centre of the universe. In the second century CE, Claudius
Ptolemy wrote his *Amalgest*, a treatise that summarised all
of the prior knowledge of astronomy from the Babylonians
and Greeks. Around the same time, the Maya in Central
America were developing their astronomical calendars and
building great pyramids aligned with the night sky.

And then the sciences went dormant in Europe. The fall
of the Roman Empire ushered in the Dark Ages and subsequent wars over several centuries, including the Crusades,
which marked a time when academic pursuits were ham-
pered. But Ptolemy's writings had quietly made their way
east via trade routes, and Persian astronomers translated
the *Amalgest*, even noting errors in Ptolemy's work. For
several centuries, Muslim astronomers were the only ones
who continued and corrected Ptolemy's work, producing
new instruments like the astrolabe, a complex device with
spinning plates that could track the movements of stars and
tell time.

In 1259, Hulagu Khan – grandson of Mongol ruler
Chinggis Khan – expanded the Mongol empire into what
is now Iran and ordered the construction of the Maragheh

Observatory, led by scientist Nasir al-Din al-Tusi. Al-Tusi compiled a star catalogue, called a zij in Persian, made updates to Ptolemy's work and put forward groundbreaking theories to describe planetary motion. About 350 years before Galileo viewed the Milky Way through a telescope, al-Tusi already had seminal ideas about the galaxy, including that the 'milky' quality was likely caused by clusters of small stars – he was right! Some scholars believe that Ulugh Beg became interested in astronomy after visiting the ruins of the Maragheh Observatory as a child and decided to establish his own observatory in Samarkand to make an accurate update to al-Tusi's star catalogue.

Ulugh Beg was one of the first astronomers to understand the importance of large, permanently mounted astronomical instruments. Up until his time, instruments were smaller and portable – astrolabes, sextants and quadrants that could be carried. His massive, stationary quadrant literally carved into the Samarkand hillside was the first of its kind. This type of solid, earth-bound instrument could produce much more accurate measurements because it was immovable.

But by far his greatest contribution to astronomy was the *Zij-i Sultani*, an astronomical table that catalogued the precise measurements of 1,018 stars grouped into forty-eight constellations. It contained the only new measurements of the stars carried out between the eras of Ptolemy in the second century and Danish astronomer Tycho Brahe in the sixteenth. Ulugh Beg's zij became a gold standard in star catalogues and was translated into Latin and used by

European astronomers several hundred years later, effectively keeping astronomy alive while Europe languished in the Dark Ages.

Ulugh Beg also measured with astounding accuracy the tilt of the Earth and the length of the solar year at 365 days, five hours, forty-nine minutes and fifteen seconds – an error of just twenty-five extra seconds – greater accuracy than some later European astronomers achieved.

After his assassination, the observatory was razed by religious extremists who didn't approve of his scientific studies. Thankfully, several of his pupils continued his work – notably Ali Qushji, who saved as many of the observatory's tools and books as he could and carried them to Istanbul, where they were stored and eventually disseminated across Europe. This is likely where, in the seventeenth century, British astronomer John Greaves purchased a copy of Ulugh Beg's zij, which he took back to Oxford, where it is still held in the Bodleian Library.

After I returned from Uzbekistan, I went to Oxford to view the manuscript. Having collected my reader's card and ascended to the library's top level, where restricted materials were kept, I was handed a small box containing the leather-bound book and told not to take flash photos. Inside were paragraphs written in beautiful Persian calligraphy and pages upon pages of charts carefully outlined in red, black and gold ink. They contained the star catalogue and charts of lunar and solar movements. I sat with it for several hours, flipping carefully through the delicate leaves, hardly able to believe I was holding a book that Ulugh Beg may have written himself almost exactly 600 years before.

After I finished the observatory tour with Saodat, I took a taxi across Samarkand to the Gur-e-Amir, the mausoleum complex of the Timurid emperors. Their empire started with Ulugh Beg's grandfather, Timur, and covered a large area of what is now Iran, Iraq, Afghanistan and Central Asia during the fifteenth century.

It was nearing midday, and the sunshine was beating down on Samarkand, which lies in a flat plain that radiates the heat like a stovetop. I paid the entry fee at a small ticket office, then walked into the main courtyard, skirting a group of domestic tourists following a tour guide with a white flag. The women were eye-catching in their long dresses with brightly coloured geometric designs, each wearing a silken headscarf in equally vivid colours with the ends flowing down over their shoulders.

The Gur-e-Amir is a staggeringly beautiful building. Classical Islamic pointed arches cover the front, with the main pishtaq entryway marked by a recessed arch filled with muqarnas – niche-like decorations that form three-dimensional stalactites resembling elaborate stars. Above rises a single, ribbed dome tiled in turquoise. This is flanked on either side by round minaret towers. The entire structure is covered in geometric mosaics in every imaginable shade of blue. I passed a guide telling a group of visitors, 'The great emperor Timur's colour of empire was blue because blue is the colour of the sky and there is nothing beyond the sky.'

Inside, the mausoleum was refreshingly cool. Imperial tombstones lined up in rows at the centre of the room, with the ceiling towering high above into a dome with more muqarnas and tiled arches. The walls were covered from floor to ceiling in carved arabesques and star-shaped geometric designs painted in gold and turquoise. The whole room seemed to shimmer.

I sat on a bench and admired the tombs. Timur's stood imposingly in the middle, rendered in black stone. Surrounding it were those of his successor-sons and, at the bottom, Ulugh Beg's took pride of place in white marble. At that moment, a small group of local tourists began singing. Their chant started as a hum, low and guttural, and rose to a crystalline high note that echoed off of the tomb's golden walls. It was angelic and moving, and though I didn't understand their words, I felt the meaning rising through my throat in a rush of tears that spilled over and splashed on the jade floor. It was a feeling of unlikely connectedness through cultures, languages, time and space. Somehow, here we all were – the Uzbek tourists, Ulugh Beg and me, joined by a song, the stars and the simple act of being human.

The next day, I met up with local guide Viktoria Yalanskaya, who had promised to take me to the modern astronomical observatory at Mount Maidanak. Maidanak is the biggest and most important optical observatory in Central Asia, situated at almost 3,000 metres above sea level at the western tip of the Pamir-Alay Mountains, some 200 kilometres southeast of Samarkand. We had a long drive ahead of us.

Viktoria arrived at my hotel a few minutes late wearing a long Uzbek suzani jacket that floated as she walked in. She apologised profusely – she hadn't been able to arrange a babysitter, so her 3-year-old daughter, Yasmine, would come with us. We piled into the back of a black SUV with a driver who introduced himself as Namos – a stocky man with a crew cut and a white-striped polo shirt.

The drive south out of the city was flat, the land spreading away like a dusty rug. Viktoria and I talked about life, tourism and nature while Yasmine snacked on dried fruits and watched cartoons on a tablet. I confessed that I was anxious about an upcoming part of my research: I would be spending four days in complete darkness on a retreat at a monastery in Germany. I needed to get as deeply as I could into the subject of darkness to really experience it, but admittedly was having reservations about surviving four days in a silent room with no light. The responses when I'd told people about the dark retreat had ranged from amazement to horror.

But Viktoria was comforting. 'Actually, this sounds very relaxing to me. Just to have nothing to do or worry about,' she said smiling at Yasmine, who had climbed onto her and was force-feeding her pistachios. 'You will rest and sleep and have so many ideas.'

We stopped briefly for lunch in Shahrisabz, another ancient Silk Road city far less visited by modern tourists. Sitting in a courtyard restaurant shaded by walnut trees, with the song of a bubbling fountain, we ate cucumber and tomato salad and samsa, meat-stuffed savoury pastries that arrived steaming from the oven. Afterwards, Viktoria showed me the tomb that Emperor Timur built for himself but never used. He died during the winter, and it was impossible to transport his body that far, so he was interred in the golden mausoleum I'd seen the day before at the Gur-e-Emir in Samarkand. Apart from a few Uzbek travellers making a pilgrimage, we were the only visitors.

Outside of the unused mausoleum, a local woman was selling bags, purses and doppa hats, all embroidered in exquisite detail with geometric and plant motifs. I bought a purse swirling with leaves and flowers in banana yellow, bright red, azure and green thread. Viktoria told me that the artist did all of the embroidery by hand. As we left, she gave us a bag full of plump, juicy cherries picked from a tree at her home.

Viktoria warned me that the road to Maidanak was bad. She had been there the year before, and it took hours to reach the top on a bumpy dirt track. The observatory is remote, and the astronomers like to keep it that way. Back at the astronomical institute in Tashkent, Shuhrat Ehgamberdiev had told me that the government wanted to develop astrotourism to allow people to see the stars, but the astronomers at the institute opposed it because they thought adding visitor infrastructure would increase light pollution and create problems for their scientific work.

'I visit many observatories and, usually, the tourism is during the daytime,' Shuhrat said. 'We don't want people knocking on the door and saying, "Open up, I would like to see the stars!" We're against this because we are working during those hours and we need a totally quiet, dark environment. Visitors bring hotels and hotels mean light pollution, which ruins our observations of the night sky.'

He said the government had asked if they wanted to modernise the road to the observatory, but the institute declined this as well, as a kind of insurance that they would not develop tourist resorts in the area. The scientists would rather drive for hours up an old Soviet dirt track than risk new light pollution.

From the flatlands southeast of Shahrisabz, we turned off on a two-lane road that followed the course of the Guzardarya, a small, rocky river that carved its way through red and orange hills. Every so often, a few single-storey homes were visible, shaded by stands of thin poplar trees. Goats and skinny horses strayed across the road.

'You can see already we're leaving modern Uzbekistan,' Viktoria said, pointing out the livestock to Yasmine, who gleefully screeched, 'Kozel!' – 'goat' in Russian. 'This area is so beautiful; they are preserving an older way of life.'

It took a couple more hours to reach our final destination: a yurt camp just below the observatory where we would spend the night. The Guzardarya continued in a ribbon of jade water that rushed through canyons the colour of rust. The only village in the valley was a collection of mud buildings where locals had vegetables and large cuts of meat hanging out for sale. We bumped past a pair of boys in baseball caps trotting along on a donkey. The track went farther and farther up, overlooking a few farms where families were growing sustenance crops and grass for their livestock.

Finally, Namos pulled into a drive where several large yurts were set up on platforms in a grass field looking east over the whole valley. We had reached 2,700 metres. The air was clear and the hillsides were a vivid green after the dusty flatlands. Beyond, a range of snow-capped peaks – the heart of the Pamir-Alay – jutted into the clouds.

The camp's owner showed us the yurt that Viktoria, Yasmine and I would share. It was made of a round, metal frame covered by sturdy canvas and heavy felt cloth. Inside, the ceiling was adorned with ikat fabrics – material dyed in a way that creates a distinct pattern – in bright colours, and a table was set low to the floor and dressed with an ikat table runner. A pile of silk pillows and blankets sat to one side – later in the evening we'd lay these out on the floor as our beds. A single bare lightbulb hung above us – somewhere outside, the petrol generator that powered it was rumbling.

It was still several hours before sunset, and we weren't due at the observatory until 8 p.m., so we sat at a picnic table watching the sunlight disappear and the shadows grow long down the mountains. Our host fired up a simple charcoal grill and began cooking skewers of mutton and vegetables for dinner. Viktoria said the sheep would have been raised by a family nearby and the meat would be extremely fresh. It was delicious and tender, and we gobbled it down accompanied by more tomato and cucumber salad, fresh apricots and a round loaf of dense Uzbek bread.

It was not yet fully dark when we arrived at the peak of Mount Maidanak. The sky was the colour of lapis lazuli, a dark-blue stone traded along the Silk Road in Ulugh Beg's time – the colour of Timur's empire. It faded into a thin, pinky-yellow band at the horizon and a crescent moon dangled to the west. There were no trees, just the telltale domes of several astronomical telescopes dotted down the slope and a vast view out across the darkening desert to the west. Everything was still.

We were met by astronomer Uktam Khafizov, who ran the observatory. He showed us to the top of the hill, where the largest telescope in Central Asia peeks out into the cosmos. A thick, metal door led into an echoing stairwell and up several storeys to an office, where another astronomer sat looking at computer screens. The brown laminate flooring and peeling wallpaper had seen better days and looked like it might have been left over from the Soviet era.

In the 1960s, when Uzbekistan was part of the Soviet Union, the Ulugh Beg Astronomical Institute needed to find a suitable site for a large telescope. After a ten-year search, Mount Maidanak was chosen. A Soviet laser station and several observational facilities were built on a neighbouring peak in the 1970s, and in the '80s came the first telescopes at Maidanak, with the largest – its 1.5-metre LOMO AZT-22 telescope, manufactured in Russia – seeing its first light in 1992, a year after Uzbek independence.

Mount Maidanak was notable for its favourable conditions, including high elevation, low wind speeds and good seeing. 'Seeing' is an astronomical term for the amount of visual turbulence in the air caused by moisture, dust or air pollution. With good seeing, stars appear very clearly in the sky. In poor seeing conditions, stars appear blurry or seem to twinkle or undulate. The stars themselves aren't moving – it's an optical illusion caused by the turbulence. Light pollution is another factor increasingly associated with poor seeing conditions. Ideally, astronomers need an unobstructed view with little noise and no artificial light to accurately analyse starlight and understand a star's location, distance and properties.

In these conditions, light emitted by a celestial object can be plotted along the electromagnetic spectrum, ranging from long radio waves to short, high-energy gamma rays. Not all light is visible to human eyes – only a small portion in the middle of the spectrum, appearing to us as the rainbow of colours we can see. Different chemical elements produce different colours, so astronomers can use starlight or the light from planets passed through what is essentially a prism to understand the chemical makeup of that planet or star. The seeing conditions at Maidanak were recently surveyed over several years and found to be among the best on Earth for optical astronomy – comparable to the world-class Paranal Observatory in Chile, home to the European Southern Observatory.

It was at the start of the Second World War that all of the astronomical observatories in the Soviet Union were quietly evacuated to remote locations in the middle of the country like Uzbekistan and the Ural Mountains. Shuhrat Ehgamberdiev told me that the Uzbek Astronomical Institute had got hold of the most sophisticated German clocks and astronomical timekeeping methods before the war, and that Tashkent was the only location that could provide the Soviet Union with the precise time for many months during the war. Seven times a day, Uzbek astronomers sent signals into the field, allowing the Soviets to keep time correctly.

Today, major observatories like Maidanak work regularly with scientists from South Korea, China, Japan, and in cooperation with other institutions and observatories all over the world. Astronomers and scientists from universities anywhere can request specific observations, and Maidanak performs those observations and sends them back for the astronomers to analyse. Information sharing of this sort, much like the International Space Station (ISS), is an example of astronomical science as a peacebuilding exercise. The ISS was formed in 1998 as a collaboration between the US, Russia, the European Space Agency (ESA), Japan and Canada, just a few decades after the Cold War. The partnership continues, with various countries contributing equipment, training and personnel, including the astronauts and cosmonauts who live on board the station together for months at a time, proving that hostilities can be put aside for the advancement of humankind's understanding of the cosmos.

In the observatory's office, Uktam pulled up a picture of a spiral galaxy onto the computer screen, which the telescope had taken a couple of months earlier. He explained that the astronomers also take test images of a black screen to compare for any errors or problems. I thought it was interesting that they used complete darkness to show the purity of the camera's imaging and flag issues with the lens. We walked up several more flights of stairs into a giant circular room where the massive AZT-22 telescope was pointed through an opening in the dome. It was several storeys high.

'In 2010, a new planet was found using this telescope,' Uktam said, his eyes shining proudly and his round cheeks spread into a smile. 'And now, I want to introduce you to the scientist who made this discovery. My little brother, Bahodir.' I shook the astronomer's hand and congratulated him on finding the planet, which was named 'Samarkand' in homage to Ulugh Beg.

The telescope has come a long way since it was first invented in the seventeenth century. Although no one is completely certain about who the original inventor was, in 1608 a spectacle maker in the Netherlands named Hans Lipperhey debuted a lens-based instrument that could make far-away objects seem closer. Galileo heard about it and, two years later, made his own telescope, which he used to look up at the night sky. His findings included Jupiter's four largest moons, which are not visible to the naked eye – Io, Europa, Ganymede and Callisto, often referred to now as the 'Galilean moons'. Using the telescope, he also concluded that our Moon was not perfectly spherical, and that the Earth revolved around the Sun and not the other way around, as people then thought. In 1616, Galileo was subjected to the Inquisition and banished by the Catholic Church for this teaching, which it considered heretical. Of course, we know today that Galileo was correct, but it took the Church until 1992 – 376 years – to formally pardon him.

Over the centuries, telescopes were refined, expanded and computerised. Ancient astronomers knew of the five brightest planets – Mercury, Venus, Mars, Jupiter and Saturn – because they can easily be seen with the naked eye. In the eighteenth century, German–British astronomer William Herschel discovered Uranus through a homemade telescope in his back garden in Bath. In 1846, astronomers at the Berlin Observatory first saw Neptune through the Fraunhofer telescope, and in 1930, Clyde Tombaugh found the ninth planet, Pluto (sadly demoted to 'dwarf planet' in 2006), using a telescope at Lowell Observatory in Flagstaff, Arizona.

In 1990, we figured out how to put a telescope into space, launching the Hubble Space Telescope, which is still orbiting Earth, sending back astounding images of the universe. And in December 2021, we launched the largest-ever space telescope – James Webb (JWST) – which orbits the Sun 1.5 million kilometres away from Earth. The JWST continues to send back the highest-resolution images of the universe ever taken, providing regular new insights into its origins. And there are more to come. The Nancy Grace Roman Space Telescope is scheduled to launch in 2027 and will have a wider field of view, plus the ability to take pictures of exoplanets – planets orbiting stars beyond our solar system – for the very first time.

Each of these achievements in science has become a building block for the next generation. Still, I couldn't help but feel that Ulugh Beg's observations, done purely with his own eyes and the faint starlight that fell onto his giant quadrant in Samarkand, were somehow the most impressive. The level of understanding that early astronomers had about what they were seeing and how the solar system works seems almost supernatural to me. With no context, no pictures, and no astronauts aboard the International Space Station snapping photos and giving guitar performances via phone screens, Ulugh Beg had only his eyes, his mind and a very, very dark sky full of stars.

Night had fully set in when we emerged from the Maidanak telescope's dome, and it was cold. I was glad I had worn my thermals and zipped my puffy coat up to my chin.

'You can see the air is even clearer now than it was before

sunset,' Uktam said, explaining that the desert dust, which gets whipped up during the day, settles after dark when there is less wind. 'About two hours after sunset, we start to get optimal seeing conditions up here.'

Apart from a few distant dots of light on the mountain-sides below us – probably from scattered homes with petrol generators – there was no artificial light. The sky was ablaze with stars. Uktam began pointing out constellations, reciting the names in Russian and Uzbek, with Viktoria doing her best to translate to English. I showed them an app I use with augmented reality that allows you to point your phone at the sky and learn about the objects you're seeing. Yasmine huddled close to her mum, teetering around in her pink coat, looking up.

'We've never been stargazing, so this is Yasmine's first time seeing the night sky properly. We can't see it very well in Samarkand because there is now too much light pollution,' Viktoria said.

At that moment, a white light blazed across the sky, leaving a sparkly trail behind. Yasmine squealed with delight, pointing a chubby finger at the sky.

'Oh, what *was* that?' Viktoria gasped, and Uktam explained that it was a meteor, sometimes inaccurately called a falling star.

'This is not in fact a star. It happens when a small piece of dust or a rock from space enters into Earth's atmosphere and burns up on the way down,' he said.

'Oh my god, it's my first time seeing this,' Viktoria

replied, cooing at Yasmine with excitement. Before we could catch our breath, a second meteor streaked overhead and we all laughed. I told Viktoria that she and Yasmine were lucky – meteors can be hard to spot, and you need to be in a very dark location to see them.

We fell silent for a few minutes, craning our heads up. Then Uktam pointed to one of the stars just overhead.

'Do you see this one? It is almost 600 light years away. 1 light year is the amount of time it takes light to travel one Earth year. We are looking back in time. So the light from that star entering our eyes tonight left the star six hundred years ago. The light started its journey when Ulugh Beg was alive.'

It was well after midnight when we got back to the yurt camp and Viktoria and Yasmine went straight to sleep. After I'd laid out my bedding, I went back outside and pulled a chair to an open spot overlooking the green valley I'd seen during the day. Now it was a dark expanse. The cloudy stripe of the Milky Way was rising, outlining the distant mountains. It was silent, cold, dark. The kind of sky Ulugh Beg would have known.

On my final night in Uzbekistan, the sun set over Samarkand in orange, then purple. I walked from my hotel down a narrow street through the old town to the Registan, the heart of this city at the crossroads of the Silk Road, a crucial central point on the vast stretch of the Kyzylkum Desert that travellers endured between the last Chinese oasis at Turpan and the glittering metropolises of Iran, India and, eventually, the Mediterranean.

'Registan' is a Persian word meaning 'sandy desert', and during Ulugh Beg's time, it was a dusty square with a thriving bazaar where fabrics, spices, jade and paper were exchanged, public announcements were made and executions were held.

I wove through groups of families out for an evening stroll, children playing with flashing spinners and yoyos, vendors selling balloons and bags of sweetcorn and roasted chestnuts. The main square was ticketed entry but was visible for free from a set of marble steps at its southern end. Many gathered here to sit on the stairs and take in the scene – three huge, mosaic-covered madrasas, each with a tall iwan portal arch opening into the central plaza. In the evening, they were lit up with spotlights and the entire square shimmered.

I paid the entry fee and went inside. The Ulugh Beg Madrasa was still open, though it was nearing 8 p.m. I found the central open-air courtyard lined with pointed-arch doorways, which led into former classrooms, now occupied by artists and craftspeople selling souvenir artworks, Arabic names painted in swirling calligraphy, colourful ceramics and embroidered bags. I sat on a bench and waited for a while, watching the sky darken through the courtyard's trees and trying to imagine the astronomical studies carried out there six centuries before.

The sky would have been very dark over the Registan

then. The spotlights illuminating the madrasas today would have driven a stargazer like Ulugh Beg – or me – crazy. Later on, I moved to the steps of the Sher-Dor and gazed across the square back to Ulugh Beg's Madrasa, which he had covered in mosaics of a starry night sky. The Moon was setting between the portal and the minaret tower. A few stars poked through overhead, but the spotlights, which had changed from a gentle golden glow into a purple, green and pink light show, drowned out the night sky.

During my visit to the Ulugh Beg Observatory, when I asked Saodat how medieval astronomers had figured so many things out, she said it was because they had so much access to the sky. It was dark. There was no pollution. They spent their evenings looking up at the stars and noticing tiny details, shifts, changes and patterns that we simply cannot see today because there is so much light.

Human understanding of the cosmos, and of ourselves, was born from the dark. And Ulugh Beg's work in Samarkand was crucial to the evolution of astronomy – a bridge from the ancient Greek knowledge of the sky to modern science.

Before I got up to leave, the crescent moon dipped below the madrasa and disappeared.

6

Cosmos

The Himalaya

I noticed the smell of the butter lamps first: a heavy, sweet fragrance, somehow both floral and musty. It was coming from a chest-high metal box enclosed by glass windows that had fogged up and were covered in a thin film of soot. Twenty flames flickered blurrily inside – candles made from yak butter.

Around me, a small courtyard was surrounded by stone buildings with walls painted burgundy, and overhead a clear, cobalt-blue sky was filling up with stars. I tried to take a deep breath but, at more than 3,500 metres, the air was thin and my lungs struggled. I couldn't tell if the dizziness was from the sweet, butter-lamp smoke or the lack of oxygen.

A monk emerged from the shadows dressed in crimson robes and a fleece jacket, which seemed to match the red walls, plus white Crocs on his feet and a pair of round spectacles. He smiled wordlessly and motioned for me to follow him up a set of stairs and through a wooden doorway, sliding off the Crocs as he went inside. I had to stop awkwardly to untie my shoes and take them off, then padded up the freezing stone steps in my socks, into the dukhang – the monastery's main assembly hall.

The monk switched on a set of electric lights and pointed to the walls covered in frescoes of serene-faced buddhas, bodhisattvas and mountainous landscapes. Speaking in the local Ladakhi language, he explained the meanings of the various scenes while my host, Nikki, translated. The paintings represented the different reincarnations and future life of the Buddha, as well as other auspicious symbols. Dating to the 1500s, they were painted in vermilion, blue and yellow made from natural pigments of cinnabar, lapis lazuli and saffron.

Not many people get to visit Phyang Monastery at night. It is only open to tourists during the day, but visitors like me, who come to stargaze at the monastery's small astronomy centre, the Cosmohub, are offered special access to the dukhang after the sun goes down.

The night I met with Uktam Khafizov on Mount Maidanak in Uzbekistan, he had said something that stuck with me: that looking at the stars was looking back in time because of the distance the starlight had travelled. For one star that he pointed out, the photons, or light particles entering our eyes had left the star when Ulugh Beg was still alive 600 years ago.

In the grand scheme of the cosmos, 600 years barely registers as a blip in spacetime. Our galaxy alone is thought to be about 100,000 light years across, while the edge of the observable universe is around 46.5 billion light years away in every direction and expanding. Truly unfathomably big.

Trying to wrap my mind around the scale of it all made me itchy, and I felt a deep pull to get up high. Like, *really* high. As close to outer space as possible. Luckily, I had some friends in high places – in Ladakh, the northernmost region of India up in the Himalayan Mountains. This was what had brought me to Phyang Monastery.

I'd met Sonal Asgotraa through her work as the founder of Astrostays, a community-based tourism initiative that was training homestay owners, many of them women, in the remotest parts of Ladakh. They learn basic astronomy and telescope use and then travellers can book an experience that involves staying with the family at their house, trying home-cooked food and, after the sun goes down, learning about the stars. Astrostays then partnered with Phyang Monastery to create the Cosmohub, which houses a little museum focusing on Tibetan cosmology and modern astronomy, a kitchen for local meals, and telescopes for stargazing.

I'd been keen for a while to visit Ladakh and see how the concept was working in person, and it seemed like the perfect chance to contemplate the scale of the cosmos. It was as close as I'd get to *out there* down here on Earth.

I flew into Delhi on a hot spring day, with summer not yet raging but temperatures already pushing 40 °C. Before the domestic flight up to Ladakh, I had a stop to make in Delhi at the Jantar Mantar. This astronomical observatory was one of five built in the 1720s by the Maharaja of Jaipur, and I was especially interested in the Shastansh Yantra, a large sextant enclosed in a chamber where light flows in through small holes in a brass sheet, used to determine the altitude of the sun.

The Shastansh Yantra, whose design is based on Ulugh Beg's Observatory, is the closest approximation to what it would have looked like if it was still standing in Samarkand today. The Maharaja Jai Singh II also used Ulugh Beg's zij star catalogue as the basis for his own updated version. Another instrument at the observatory, the Rama Yantra, consists of a pair of cylindrical structures with windows, an open top and a central pillar used to mark the angles of celestial objects. Its design, with three circular storeys of arched windows, reminded me very much of the drawings I'd seen imagining the Samarkand observatory before it was razed. And like Ulugh Beg's Observatory, the Jantar Mantar was built on a north–south axis, which was important for obtaining accurate measurements.

It stands in a quiet park next to the bustling concentric roundabouts of Connaught Place, Delhi's busy financial and tourist district. I was the only visitor and walked around sweating in the humidity, thinking about how Ulugh Beg's ideas had migrated more than 1,500 kilometres across South

Asia. It would have taken more than a month then to travel between Samarkand and Delhi by foot, camel or horse.

Touching down the next day in Ladakh's capital city, Leh, was a relief from Delhi's raging heat. I was met by Simar Preet Kaur, who oversees Astrostays' operations, along with local coordinator Nikki Stanzing Yangskit. The streets of Leh were cluttered with cars, donkey carts, wandering cattle and construction dust. Just outside of town, we passed a big military base teeming with green army trucks. In the distance in every direction were the arid peaks of the Himalayas, topped with snow.

To quickly sketch the geography: the Himalayan range runs in a south-eastward curve from Pakistan to China, passing through India, Nepal and Bhutan along the way. The Pamir-Alay Mountains, where I had been stargazing on Mount Maidanak in Uzbekistan, form the northern reaches of this vast ridgeline, which culminates on Qomolangma, or Mount Everest – the highest peak on Earth at 8,849 metres. The entire region, including the Himalayan mountains and its many countries, communities and cultures, is referred to as 'the Himalaya' – a singular geocultural term that attempts to capture the whole region and its diversity of landscapes and people.

Ladakh is part of Kashmir, an area of long dispute between India, Pakistan and China. The conflict over Kashmir started with the partition of India in 1947 and resulted in three wars and multiple armed skirmishes between India and Pakistan, most recently in early 2025, with both sides staking full claim to the entire region, and China elbowing in for territory in the east. The story is a complex one of decades of violent massacres, political jostling and outright war, very little of it involving the input or best interests of the Indigenous Kashmiri people.

In 1971, the Line of Control was established, which continues to serve as a de facto border separating the Azad Kashmir and Gilgit–Baltistan regions in Pakistan-controlled territory to the north, from Ladakh and the J&K (Jammu and Kashmir) territory on the Indian side to the south. Although J&K continues to experience some violence, most of Ladakh is stable and sees a growing number of tourists each summer, mainly mountain trekkers, backpackers and spiritual seekers visiting the region's Tibetan Buddhist monasteries.

This wasn't my first visit to this part of the world. A few years earlier I had gone to Mount Everest through Tibet. Getting there involved days of travelling slowly higher and higher. First, by overnight train on the world's highest railway, from Qinghai province to Lhasa, the capital of Tibet.

The Qinghai–Tibet Railway is a dreamy travel proposition, trundling for fourteen hours across high, barren land and arid mountain passes that top 5,000 metres. For a little while, you gaze at the ice-blue waters of Qinghai Lake – China's largest – and if you're lucky you might catch the fleeting blur of a herd of Tibetan antelope racing away. Once night falls, you lie back in your sleeper bunk, lulled by the rocking of the rails, and stare up out of a frosty window at an inky sky, where constellations of stars are outlined by mountain shadows passing ever onward into the night.

From Lhasa, several days of driving took me first to the town of Gyantse, 4,000 metres up. After that to Shigatse, where crimson-robed monks wandered in and out of dusty shops selling golden Buddhas and rolls of colourful prayer flags flapping on the thinnest breeze. And then Shegar – a windy truckstop with a row of spinning prayer wheels pointing the way to the top of the planet. Finally, Mount Everest came into view: a perfect snow-tipped triangle of rock jutting into the clouds.

Most of us know Mount Everest by its Anglophone name, applied by the Royal Geographical Society in 1865 to honour Sir George Everest, a British surveyor who never even saw the peak. But Tibetans call this mountain Qomolangma, which means 'Holy Mother', and revere her as a goddess.

In Earth terms, Qomolangma is the highest point. Her tippy-top is as close to the stars as a person can get while still standing on this planet. Though when measured from the sea floor, Mauna Kea on Hawai'i is technically Earth's tallest mountain, Qomolangma reaches up into the atmosphere more than twice as high as Mauna Kea.

The Tibet base camp below the North Face sits at 5,200 metres, an elevation at which most humans cannot breathe properly due to the thin atmosphere containing fewer oxygen molecules. To understand why oxygen is so rare at high elevations, we first have to know that Earth orbits the Sun in the so-called 'habitable zone'. This is an area of any solar system that's ideal for a planet to have liquid water and, therefore, the potential for life. This is because we are not so close to the star that we burn up and not so far that we freeze; it's the Goldilocks of orbits.

So, on Earth we have the luxury of a near-impossibility: liquid oceans, the likes of which have not been found on any other planet so far. At sea level, the conditions are right to make a magic ratio of oxygen molecules to atmospheric pressure. This alchemy keeps oxygen dense, creating the ideal conditions for life and respiration. The higher you rise away from Earth's surface and out into the atmosphere, the less air pressure there is as oxygen molecules spread out and there are fewer of them for your lungs to gather up in each breath.

Aside from air travel in pressurised planes, there aren't many places in the world as high as Qomolangma that humans can go, and there are almost no permanent settlements this high.

But in the scheme of our solar system, Qomolangma is dwarfed by another mountain: Olympus Mons, the highest point on Mars. There is no taller mountain on any other body orbiting our Sun. Olympus Mons is a volcano, which was piled up to a whopping 24 kilometres high by the millennia of lava flows and ash that formed the once-living Red Planet. It juts from the surface of Mars more than two-and-a-half times the height of Qomolangma.

Diagrams comparing the two show a teeny, snow-capped Qomolangma overshadowed by a lumbering Olympus Mons, so wide it barely looks like a mountain. Its caldera alone is 85 kilometres across, and if it were plonked on Earth, it would cover almost the entirety of France. This is truly something given how small Mars is – about half the size of Earth.

My drive into Everest Base Camp was on a pristine Chinese road engineered in almost impossibly delicate conditions, not unlike the Qinghai–Tibet Railway, which runs on track laid through permafrost. The road ascends over curving switchbacks and through a high tundra that stretches bare, brown and treeless in every direction. We zoomed up the empty highway and Qomolangma spiked into view – a jagged slice of frost-covered shale at the top of a glacial valley.

At the base camp, I stepped out of the car and immediately struggled to breathe. Even walking across a flat surface felt like carrying weights around my legs – the opposite of what I imagined astronauts Neil Armstrong and Buzz Aldrin must've felt as they first bounced around the Moon at one-sixth the gravity of Earth. I made my way slowly to a boulder and sat inhaling shallow gulps of rarefied air, watching the sun set behind the peak, which cast an eerie, Everest-shaped shadow down the long valley of rock scree.

That night, I slept in one of the 'tent hotels' set up by locals at the base camp, although several months after my visit, the Tibetan side of Everest was closed to overnight visitors and the tent hotels were shut down due to concerns about the area's delicate ecosystem.

The tent I stayed in was owned by a Tibetan woman named Dolkar, who ran her hotel with crisp efficiency, cooking all of the meals while looking after three young children, keeping fires going, brewing tea and tending to guests. In the evening, I sat cross-legged on a banquette made of pillows and Dolkar prepared me a steaming bowl of noodle soup with yak meat and poured a cup of sweet, milky tea from a huge tin flask.

During the night, I lay restless in the dark. Oxygen deprivation also affects your sleep, and I was staving off a mild panic. A normal, sea-level body can acclimatise to life at 4,000 and even 5,000 metres after a few days or weeks. I was at 5,200 and had taken a tablet to help with altitude adjustment. Anywhere above 7,500 metres is referred to as the 'death zone' because so little oxygen enters the body that the organs can quickly go into failure, which is why it's such a feat when a climber reaches the top of Everest without an oxygen tank, as Polish climber Piotr Krzyżowski did in May 2024.

By 3 a.m., the tent's central stove had gone out, I needed a wee and the temperature had dropped to −15 °C outside. Cold temperatures are another effect of the low air pressure at high elevations and further proof that life on Earth is seemingly miraculous. It's only because of the planet's improbably liveable atmospheric pressure, thanks to its ideally placed orbit, that we are all here, breathing, stargazing, cycling, swimming, falling in love and writing books.

Outside the tent, the waxing moon was up, illuminating the mountain into a cool, white triangle above the valley. As my boots crunched across the gravel to the outhouse, I anticipated the unfortunate smells and frigid squatting manoeuvres, and I was deeply wishing I did not have to go. Every step felt laboured: skin pulled tight over bones and head in a vice grip. But there was also magic.

Qomolangma is often covered in clouds. During the day, the mountain creates her own weather. Clouds form as slightly warmer air rises off the surface of the peak and mixes with condensation in the atmosphere. From far away, she appears like a steaming volcano with a white storm constantly swirling over her crown. But at night, the peak's surface temperature stays cold enough that clouds don't form. This bit of meteorology also explains why evening flights are less turbulent and why nighttime often seems clearer and calmer than daytime. There is literally less weather at night.

I followed the line of the Milky Way running in a shining river perpendicular to the mountain. Standing under this firmament, wheezing and shivering, my eyes took in more and more starlight. For each moment, it seemed another star appeared where there wasn't one before. Two stars, Arcturus and Spica, were there like familiar friends I knew from the skies above London, but with no light pollution for hundreds of miles, they got lost among so many more stars and so much moonlight.

I fell in love with the Himalaya on that trip and vowed

to see as much of the region as I could, later visiting other culturally Tibetan parts of China in Qinghai, Gansu and Sichuan. So, this trip to Ladakh was fulfilling an ongoing dream.

The first twenty-four hours at high elevations require still-ness and rest as your body adjusts to less oxygen. Simar and Nikki drove me to my Ladakh homestay, a farmhouse in a steep-sided valley west of Leh. I could see the monastery from my bedroom windows on a nearby hilltop, with its burgundy walls and golden roofs. Downstairs, my host-ess was introduced as 'Ache' (pronounced like ach-ay), a Ladakhi honorific that means 'elder sister'. Dressed in a pink headscarf, a wool jumper and a blue puffy coat, she mo-tioned for me to sit on the living room banquette covered in oriental rugs and began making butter tea using a traditional tea churn – a wooden cylinder in which tea, butter and salt are mixed with a plunger. The tea was salty and oily and tasted very comforting. Her two young children played with a toy truck and talked to me in Ladakhi, not worried about whether we could understand each other.

My total-darkness retreat was now looming only a few weeks away. Anytime I thought about it, I got a pit in my stomach. In the evening, I texted my best friends Lauren and Summer and told them I was worrying about it. What if I couldn't hack it and had to come out early? What if I had a breakdown? Summer wrote back and reminded me there was no way to know what it would be like or how I would feel until I was in the thick of it. If darkness was emptiness, then what I projected into it was important. I decided from then on I would embody my Uzbek friend Viktoria and project rest, calm and creativity into the retreat, not fear.

That night, I stood on the balcony outside my room and looked at the stars through a stand of poplar trees that were still leafless in the cold spring air. The mountains formed a black outline, and the crisp night smelled like the one I'd spent at Qomolangma, earthy yet featherlight. The stars felt very close. Almost like I might reach out and touch one.

The following morning, we went to the nearby village of Choglamsar to the Ladakh Dharma Centre – a non-denominational temple at which lamas, monks and nuns from all three main branches of Buddhism can gather. That day they were holding a bumskor, a ceremony where lamas come from fourteen areas of Ladakh to pray for world peace and create good energy. Lamas poured out from the golden-roofed main hall in a sea of crimson and saffron-coloured robes, some wearing floppy maroon hats indicating they were from the 'red hat' sects; others had on Ray-Ban sunglasses and baseball caps.

Inside, we followed locals making spiritual offerings, moving through the temple in a clockwise direction towards a large seated golden Buddha statue. Nikki joined the other devout who were prostrating at the entrance, lowering her entire body until her forehead reached the floor, with arms and legs spread out.

Circumambulation, or making a clockwise pilgrimage

around a temple, sacred structure, or even the base of the holy Mount Kailash in Tibet, is an integral part of Buddhist practice. The clockwise direction is an adaptation of a Sanskrit term for 'sun-wise', meaning the early lamas circumambulated following the Sun's course through the sky, with sacred structures like stupas and temples built in alignment with sunrise and sunset.

Hanging from every beam and pole were prayer flags. Nikki explained that the five colours – blue, white, red, green and yellow – symbolised the cosmic elements of the sky, air, fire, water and earth, and that when someone was ill, they would rub a prayer flag on their head and hang it in a higher place for healing.

She explained the basic tenets of Buddhist cosmology. 'In every aspect of life, we are ascending. Even monks sit at a higher place in the temple the more they learn. So, we are all going higher and higher. This is part of our culture.'

Cosmology is a word that can be applied either to the scientific study of the origins of the universe or to a spiritual belief system about creation and where life comes from. For example, in Christian cosmology, God created everything with Earth at the centre of the universe and God, heaven and hell in fixed places. Buddhist cosmology is among the most complex of any religion, describing in detail the shape and evolution of the universe across six vertical planes of existence, with the higher planes reserved for those who have reincarnated many times and achieved higher states of spirituality.

In one sutra, or scripture, the Buddha spoke about darkness, describing how there are 'world intervals, vacant and boundless, regions of gloom and impenetrable darkness where the light of the Sun and Moon, so powerful and mighty, does not reach'. It is tantalising to compare this ancient Buddhist teaching about vast dark reaches of the universe to what is now known by modern physics: all the things we can see and measure – all matter, light, solar systems, planets, radio waves, X-rays, stars and galaxies – *everything* – makes up just 5 per cent of the whole universe. The other 95 per cent is comprised of two strange 'dark' forces.

Dark matter and dark energy, two semi-related concepts at the cutting edge of astrophysics, are pushing the boundaries of what scientists know about the universe and how it works, both on a cosmic and an atomic scale.

Back in London, I'd met with Dr Harry Cliff, a particle physicist who works at the Large Hadron Collider at CERN, to try to get a handle on what these terms mean. He suggested we grab a drink at an artsy pub in south London and, before we even sat down, he launched into an animated discussion about what we know about dark matter and dark energy, describing them as 'mysterious substances' that are invisible to us.

Evidence for dark matter was discovered by the American astronomer Vera Rubin in the 1970s, when she found that some galaxies were spinning so fast that, according to the known laws of physics, their stars should be flying off into outer space. She reasoned that there must be something generating enough extra gravity to keep the stars attached to their galaxies. This invisible stuff was termed dark matter.

Dark energy is slightly different. Although thanks to the work of US astronomer Edwin Hubble, we've known since 1929 that the universe is expanding; it was always thought that this process was slowing down. The idea was that, after the Big Bang, the universe continued to expand outward, but slower and slower over time, due to gravity's tendency to pull everything together. But in the 1990s, astronomers were looking at the light from exploding stars and realised that the receding light appeared to be moving away more rapidly.

The universe was actually speeding up.

According to Cliff, the best current explanation for this is 'a strange form of energy that permeates all of space, generating a repulsive force that overwhelms gravity at sufficiently large distances and drives the universe to expand faster and faster'. Astrophysicists call this force dark energy.

The explanations for these two phenomena, dark matter in particular, are among the most intriguing theories in modern science, with astronomers from all over the world studying them. At the UK's National Astronomy Meeting I'd met an astronomer from the University of Notre Dame, Dr John LoSecco, who believed he'd found evidence for dark matter 'objects' by studying signals from pulsars – spinning neutron stars that emit beams of electromagnetic radiation at extremely regular intervals – 'the atomic clocks of space', as he called them. He said that if one of these super-regular pulses arrives a split-second later than expected, we know it was interrupted by something along its path to Earth. After ruling out all other known possibilities, LoSecco was fairly sure he'd found a collection of something that could be called dark matter that was responsible for slowing the pulses.

Cliff told me the label 'dark' is slightly confusing because dark matter isn't exactly dark, it's invisible. 'It's decoupled from the realm of electromagnetism and light and radio waves and all the rest of it. So it lives in some other kind of reality. We don't know whether our reality makes contact with it apart from through gravity.'

In this sense, the term 'dark' has more of a philosophical meaning – dark matter is the ultimate unknown stuff of the universe. And Cliff thinks the metaphorically 'dark' stuff – the unknowns – are the most exciting parts of science, so much so that he wrote an entire book about anomalies in physics, called *Space Oddities*.

'The thing that makes science exciting is this process of discovery,' he told me as we finished our drinks. 'So when you get to an unknown area, that's exciting. It's like trying to reveal what's in that darkness.'

It struck me that I'd been thinking a lot about how humans fear and even vilify dark and unknown things. I'd also been reckoning with my own anxieties about darkness in the lead-up to the dark room retreat – it felt as if it might expose me to myself and show my weaknesses to the world. But in a scientific context, the dark unknown offers the best conditions for discovery. This sense of curiosity was the energy I needed to take into the room.

After the lama gathering, Nikki and Simar took me back to Leh to visit a local astrologer, Rigzin Angdus, more often called Onpo, a Ladakhi honorific for astrologers. Onpo is an assistant professor of medicinal astrology at India's National Institute of Sowa Rigpa, or traditional Tibetan medicine. Sowa Rigpa is a holistic approach to health incorporating physical therapies, herbs, lifestyle and the study of the stars and planets. Onpo practises the latter, using knowledge about how a person's date of birth, together with the alignment of planets, is believed to impact their personalities and life paths.

There is tension nowadays between those studying the science of outer space – astronomers – and those who believe the stars and planets have some effect on human life – astrologers. Most Western astronomers consider astrology a pseudoscience at best and want no association with it, but as I'd learned in Uzbekistan, modern astronomy was built on human curiosity about the stars and how they were thought to affect our lives here on Earth. Most early astronomers, including Ulugh Beg, as well as the granddad of astronomy, Galileo, practised astrology in some form or another, divining information and predictions from the cosmos for emperors and the rich. I recalled that Ulugh

Beg was even said to have predicted his own date of death using astrology.

Onpo told me that the practice of astrology is very much a part of everyday life in Ladakh. People regularly consult their family astrologer for life decisions on everything from the right time to get married to the precise time of day to purchase a new car. An activity or life event scheduled at the wrong time, astrologically speaking, could have disastrous results or negative effects on one's physical health or future life events.

This follows ancient astronomical practices from every region of Ladakh. For example, traditionally, people in the Changtang region were nomadic, using the stars to decide how and when to move to different places. Or in the Sham region, different household tasks were done according to the movements of the Sun, Moon and stars. When sunlight reflected off a certain part of a specific hill, people knew they could start ploughing the field or moving manure.

The birth charts that Onpo studies show where the Sun, Moon and planets were in the sky when a person was born, as well as which of the five elements are strong or weak for them. These connect the human body to the stars according to a system created by ancient Tibetans, a medical astrology that predicts where the five elements may be imbalanced. If an individual born in a certain year and month has lots of fire and heat in their chart, Onpo will then prescribe a medicine, herb or lifestyle practice to help balance out the fire and 'cool' the body.

'Our body is made up of the five elements, and the food or medicine we take is also made up of these five elements,' he said. 'So we look at the stars and at which element is low or missing for someone. According to that, we'll give a medicine that has the element they need.'

Onpo told me modern astrologers rarely go out and look at the night sky now, but instead rely heavily on the knowledge collected by people who historically had regular access to a dark sky and understood the movements of the stars.

'I am lucky. I have friends with telescopes, and they took me out to look at the stars.' He smiled at Nikki and Simar, who said they'd recently taken him out stargazing. 'It completely changed how I felt about the stars. For me, I'm usually looking at books and a laptop. It was amazing to be reminded that the stars are real; we can see them every night in Ladakh.'

'Over here, do you see this group of stars close to the top of the mountains?' said Dorjey, Astrostays' lead stargazing guide, as he pointed excitedly toward the western horizon. My favourite star cluster, Pleiades, was almost setting behind the Himalayas. 'In Ladakh, these stars are called Min-duk, which means "six stars". With telescopes, we know there are a lot more stars than six, but our ancestors could only see six with their eyes, so they called it Min-duk.'

We were standing in front of the Cosmohub, the cabin-like structure the monks at Phyang Monastery had agreed to let Astrostays use as an astronomy centre. It was run by five women from the local village who prepared traditional meals, led stargazing sessions and held cultural exchanges with visitors who signed up for their evening events. The temperature was hovering at freezing and Dorjey explained the constellations while Tashi – the keenest stargazer among the village ladies – was aiming a large telescope at a distant galaxy.

Min-duk, our old friend the Pleiades, was important to Ladakhi farmers, who used the asterism as a guide to sowing their crops when it set in the spring. Likewise, when they saw it rising again in the east, that signalled autumn was arriving – time for the harvest season. I couldn't help but note the similarities between the Ladakhi farmers' use of the Pleiades and the Māori people, who built their entire calendar around the constellation, setting their new year at the Pleiades' annual rising. It seemed everywhere I went, there was a different local name and significance for this particular group of stars, that it had helped people understand and track Earth's annual cycles and seasons for all of human history.

I asked if there were any other Ladakhi names and stories for different stars, and Dorjey explained that the constellation Europeans call Scorpius (the scorpion) is known in Ladakh as Laksor, a giant hand with a curled pinky finger rather than a tail. His grandparents had told him if the Moon passed closer to the pinky finger it would be a good year for dairy because Ladakhis have the habit of checking for spoiled milk by dipping their pinky finger into the milk jug. But if the Moon passed closer to the other fingers, it would be a bad year because fingers hold a knife to cut meat, and Buddhists traditionally eschew the use of knives as being too violent. If the Moon passed somewhere in the middle, near the wrist, it would be a bountiful harvest because Ladakhi farmers carry their harvest baskets on their forearms.

Later, we sat inside the Cosmohub warming up with bowls of thukpa, a noodle soup prepared by the women of the village. Nikki told me that the knowledge of the night sky was disappearing in Ladakh. 'Even in Changtang, where lots of people knew the tales of the sky, that knowledge vanished.' Dorjey said only his grandparents still knew the Ladakhi names of some constellations, but the younger generation was completely cut off from them because they had moved to the city and lost their connection to the stars. Dorjey, Tashi and the team were working to gather as many of their Ladakhi names and stories as they could from the older generation, to keep the knowledge alive.

On my final evening in Ladakh, I stayed at a hotel in Leh. The room had a big balcony overlooking the town from the north. I put on a thick jumper and sat outside watching the sky darken. As the day faded away, thick grey storm clouds that had been hovering over the peaks to the south eased off, revealing their snowy tops. The town spread out below and street lamps began to twinkle through the dusk.

A bright set of lights illuminated Leh Palace, the historic

royal edifice built to look like the famous Potala Palace in Tibet. It sat proudly on a bare hillside overlooking the old town and cast a surreal glow down the mountain. Below, a few hotels and a Buddhist stupa were also brightly lit up. I thought about the young Ladakhis that Dorjey had said were moving to the city and losing their connection to the natural sky. Still, I couldn't help but feel a sense of hope that the work the Astrostays team was doing would help save some of the traditional Ladakhi knowledge of the stars.

As cosmologist Carl Sagan said, 'The cosmos is within us. We are made of star stuff. We are a way for the universe to know itself.' And whether you love or hate astrology, it remains true that everything in the universe, including our bodies, is built of the same chemicals that blasted out of exploding stars. We are all made up of universal elements. We have evolved over millennia according to the laws of physics and the day-night cycle we experience here on Earth. Meeting Onpo and learning how Ladakhis connect the sky to people's lives made me want to dive further into experiencing the night. It was time to go into the dark for real.

7

Shadow Work

Germany

I awoke in the pitch black. All was silent. I blinked my eyes a few times, but open or closed, everything was the same: complete darkness. For a few moments, I lay disoriented and unsure where I was; then it came flooding back.

I was in the dark room.

I'd arrived the afternoon before on a train that crossed the countryside of northern Germany, past farmlands high with summer grass, and alighted at a tiny stop called Bobitz. There was nothing but a one-room station building that was closed. A man in a black uniform was waiting for me beside a van with the words *Kloster Gut Saunstorf – Ort der Stille* scrawled in gold lettering across the door. We drove a couple of miles up the road and pulled into a circular drive in front of a yellow, neoclassical manor house with a grand set of stairs leading up to the entrance. Deep in the basement of this villa, I would shut myself in the dark for four days.

Germany hadn't always been the plan. When I was outlining this book, my friend and fellow shadow-seeker, Kimbers, told me about a spiritual centre in Guatemala where she'd done a treehouse retreat. They had a cave room where you could go and spend time in the dark. Online, I watched videos of people there emerging blindfolded and happy-sobbing from their dark retreats to view the sunrise over a jungle-fringed lake. That seemed like the right sort of location for the book I envisioned myself writing, and I immediately put my name on the list. But weeks went by and, eventually, the centre got in touch to say they were closing their dark room. I would have to look elsewhere.

It turns out, there aren't many places in the world that offer dark room retreats. Maybe it's a logistical difficulty to run; there are safety considerations and, clearly, there isn't loads of demand to be shut away for days on end without a sliver of light. There was a place in Oregon with a retreat room built into a hillside in an isolated forest, but they only took on a few retreatants and had a two-year waiting list. Finally, a third option, Kloster Gut Saunstorf, offered me a spot in its dark room at just the right time. Billing itself as a 'modern monastery', the kloster was founded by a spiritual teacher named OM C. Parkin, who, as far as I could tell, had made up his own spiritual tradition loosely based on a New Age mix of Buddhist, Hindu and Christian ideas. I didn't really care, and I wasn't going there to buy their brand of spirituality wholesale. Kloster Gut Saunstorf was the only retreat centre with a dark room and an opening.

I booked it.

When I told my agent and editor my four-days-in-the-dark plan, their eyes grew wide. Other people said I was brave or expressed curiosity. One friend laughed and said he couldn't think of anything worse. Why go to such an extreme?

In his *Alchemical Studies Vol. 13*, the psychiatrist Carl Jung wrote that one does not become enlightened 'by imagining figures of light, but by making the darkness conscious'. Jung was obsessed with the idea of the 'shadow self' – a term he coined for the unknown or repressed parts of our psyches, typically including traumas, difficulties and ugly parts of ourselves that we would rather not face. Jung believed that through a type of therapy he called 'shadow work', you could explore and integrate these hidden realms of the mind and, in doing so, become the most healed and authentic version of yourself. The goal was to be aware of your pain and emotional injuries so that you wouldn't act out unconscious responses to hidden trauma.

My own path into studying darkness had begun years before. Going through the breakdown of my marriage, the death of my beloved stepfather, falling in love with someone who couldn't be with me, and being laid off from what was at the time my dream job, all in the space of about three years, sent me into a downward spiral. Talking therapy did nothing, as I sat in front of a kind-faced psychologist who offered me a tissue and suggested I make a cup of tea when it felt like things got too bad.

There was a period of depression where I nearly couldn't move, and in a moment of true despair, I decided to try out meditation. My childhood was a confusing and traumatising mix of barefoot hippieism and legalistic, US Christian schooling, and years prior, I had rejected the ideology of the evangelicalism in which I was brought up. Apart from dabbling visits to Buddhist temples on trips to China for work, I had no spiritual or mindfulness practice. I chose a guided 'emergency meditation' for someone in crisis that I found on YouTube. It took me through breathing exercises and focused on the five senses. I felt less panicked and tried again the next day. And the next. It helped.

I began to meditate in the evenings, sitting under the stars, letting my depression, childhood pain and recent heartaches melt into the sky. The stars were so far away. Their light had travelled hundreds, even thousands of years to reach me. They had seen billions of people come and go, with all their problems and wars, brokenness and sadness. Mine was a drop in the bucket.

And the stars didn't flinch or freak out or change the subject; they just let me cry, long and hard.

I also began reading about darkness in all its forms, starting with the work of sixteenth-century Spanish mystic and poet St John of the Cross. He described a phase in some people's lives that he called the 'dark night of the soul', during which one is purified by experiencing grief, confusion, helplessness and eventually an 'unselfing' – concepts that inspired Jung's ideas on shadow work. I drew comfort from the notion that others had experienced such uncertainty and pain, that this might be part of a path back to my true self, and so I carried on reading, questioning and pondering how it all connected up: the grief and pain humans would rather not face; the cosmic womb from which we are all born; the black mysteries of the universe; the night we are so afraid of; and the light switch we so often reach for in the dark.

It took several years of personal study, meditation, movement and self-prescribed time in nature – usually on very long walks through English forests – but I eventually emerged. The evening sessions under the stars no longer prompted tears. I had become comfortable enough sitting with and accepting my pain that it had started to dissipate.

The English language is filled with metaphors equating darkness and the night with bad things. 'Dark days' are times of extreme misfortune. To be 'kept in the dark' is to be given no information, and if one is 'grasping in the dark', they are lost and purposeless. A 'dark cloud on the horizon' is a bad omen. The list goes on.

Much of this negative connotation can be traced back to the Judeo-Christian tradition. The Bible is filled with metaphors likening the Christian god to 'light' while positioning his enemy – the devil – as the 'prince of darkness'. Both the Old and New Testaments in almost every version contain similar language. It starts at the very beginning, just four verses into the book of Genesis:

'God saw that the light was good, and he separated the light from the darkness.'

But other spiritual and philosophical traditions don't necessarily view darkness this way. Chinese Daoism, to take one example, is based on the principle of yin and yang, which says that all things exist as inseparable opposites that attract and complement each other, such as female-male, dark-light and old-young. These concepts cannot exist without each other and are represented by the well-known circular symbol with a white crescent and black dot intertwined with a black crescent and white dot. In this tradition, darkness and light emerge from a single life force called qi, and neither are bad or good – both are simply neutral forces of life.

Over the years, my spiritual questioning merged with my work on dark skies. I could no longer view light pollution purely as a physical, late-capitalist problem. I felt that the issue had philosophical, psychological and possibly even spiritual underpinnings – a fear of the unseen and unknown parts of ourselves.

In moments of deep honesty with myself, I was scared shitless of going into the dark room for four days. I was afraid of failure, having a mental breakdown or having to leave early and disgraced. But I also knew that to truly understand darkness and to write anything about it, I had to experience it in its purest form. And so waking up in a lightless room at a monastery in rural Germany somehow seemed exactly right – like the ultimate destination in a years-long journey into the dark.

Going into the dark is not a new concept; it has been practised by Indigenous wisdom-keepers, monks, ascetics and spiritual seekers for millennia as an act of deep listening, knowledge sharing, meditation and study of self. During my trip to Mount Everest a few years before, I had descended into an underground cave used for meditation by the Buddhist master Padmasambhava in the eighth century. There are caves all over the Himalaya in which he is said to have meditated on his travels between India and Tibet.

Entering that particular cave at the foot of Qomolangma, the air was hushed and dense with the smoke of butter lamps kept burning by the monks from Rongbuk Monastery just below Everest Base Camp. The silence was thick, muffled by miles-deep layers of Himalayan granite and glacial sediment, which made it feel like I was standing at the centre of the Earth. In that moment, the silence was deafening.

Cave meditation has ancient roots, with early evidence found in cave drawings depicting shamanistic healing practices. It has been a core practice in many religions for thousands of years, including Hinduism, Christianity, the mystical Sufi branch of Islam and, of course, Buddhism, which was founded by Siddhartha Gautama, who achieved enlightenment (an interesting choice of phrase) through meditation. Though cave meditation did not always involve extreme darkness, it was an aspect of the experience, along with isolation from the elements and distractions of the world. Even Jesus spent forty nights and days in the desert, where he overcame temptation in the dark. These spiritual masters knew something we have largely forgotten in the modern world: life takes seed and grows in the dark.

Of course, the spiritual practice of isolation does continue in some places. In Ladkah, a few weeks previously, my friend Nikki had taken me to a remote Buddhist monastery along the Indus River. The main halls were wedged into a steep valley, and she pointed out a small structure on a high stone ledge where monks would climb at all times of the year, even through heavy snow, to sit and meditate in complete isolation, away from everything, even the other monks.

But there are few places in normal life where we can experience absolute darkness, as artificial light is ever-present, and even on the darkest of nights there is usually the light of the stars and the moon, and often the glow of a distant town on the horizon. If Padmasambhava felt that the world was so frenetic in the 700s that he had to escape to a cave on the world's highest mountain, I don't know what kind of repose could cure a twenty-first-century life. A dark room in a monastic German basement seemed as good an option as any.

Modern dark retreat rooms are designed to let in no light whatsoever, not even a sliver through a window shade or a tiny LED. There are no electronics, no watches, no sunrises, no way to listen to music or podcasts, no e-readers or text messages. It is just you, your thoughts and your non-visual senses: smell, hearing, touch, taste.

As a preparatory exercise, I invited a couple of friends for a meal at Dans Le Noir, a 'dine in the dark' concept restaurant in London staffed by blind and visually impaired people. We stowed our phones and handbags in a locker near the entrance and were led into the dining room by a blind guide, who first told us to chain together by joining hands on shoulders. The room was completely dark and disorienting, as we could hear forks on plates and conversations all around us. We had to trust the guide to bring us safely through the maze of tables.

The menu was not revealed until after the meal, so our senses of smell and taste were heightened as we guessed at what we were eating.

I think mine is tofu – the consistency is a little soft. I definitely taste fennel. Do you have carrots on your plate? Anyone know what the sauce is? Oops, I've dropped my knife.

We came away from the meal with a new appreciation for the textures of our food and the way that interacting felt more relaxed. We also noticed our conversation came easily and centred on how we were feeling and dealing with this new, shared experience. No small talk. Pretension and dining etiquette were abandoned as we were uninhibited, enjoying the meal in whatever way felt most natural.

In the weeks leading up to the dark retreat, I would sometimes close my eyes and try to walk through my flat or perform basic daily tasks without my eyesight. It usually resulted in me bumping into the table or dropping the toothbrush.

The kloster sent me an email with a suggested packing and preparation list. It recommended bringing a plush toy for comfort. I went to a giant toy store and wandered the aisles, feeling each stuffed animal with my eyes closed, searching for the softest one – one whose fluffy fur I could imagine being comforted by in the dark. I picked a grey tiger cat. It struck me, wandering the aisles, that almost all of the toys were battery-operated, with flashing lights or LED 'on' switches. Finally, I picked up a packet of scented markers, which I thought I might use to create art in the dark by attempting to guess the colours based on their smells.

All the time, I kept reminding myself that I was not the first or last person who would sit in the dark. Knowing that seekers and spiritual teachers of so many faiths had done it for centuries gave me some comfort and eased my nerves in the lead-up to entering the room.

When I arrived at the kloster, I was welcomed by a man with a soothing voice who asked me to remove my shoes inside and led me downstairs, through a long corridor at the very back of the basement. A sign in the hallway warned that this was a dark room area and to keep the door closed.

My room was at the end of the corridor – a half-moon-shaped space with a single bed against one wall and exposed

brick on the rounded side. I entered first with the lights on –
there was a lounge chair, a meditation chair on the floor,
a wardrobe and a desk at the back underneath a window,
which was secured with multiple layers of metal shutters,
black–out blinds and heavy drapes.

An interior door separated the living area from the en-
tranceway and bathroom. Food would be delivered to a
table in the antechamber twice a day by a staff member, who
would knock on the outer door, and then I was to close the
inner door and knock back to let them know it was okay
to enter. They would knock again after they left. All this
to ensure not a single photon of light ever reached my eyes
throughout the four days.

In the afternoon before the retreat started, I took a walk
out of the monastery's front drive and down a long dirt lane-
way between two fields of wheat. In the distance, a church
spire poked above the trees. It was hot and the sun beat
down and I thought about the miracle of sunlight reaching
my eyes and skin, and suddenly felt deeply sad, wanting to
soak it all in during those final few minutes.

I texted my friend Summer that I was feeling trepidatious.

Honestly, it's fucking BRAVE to descend into sensory depri-
vation for four days, she replied. *It will be an exercise in mental*
health processing and self-soothing that you'll probably never get
again. There's no way this won't be transformative.

The one condition of Kloster Gut Saunstorf's dark room
experience was that you were visited each day by a spiritual
'companion' – their resident dark room counsellor. They

assured me there was no religious agenda or motivation for this other than to check on my wellbeing, process the experience and offer support if desired. I met my companion, Deva, as I was returning from my walk. She greeted me in the monastery's main meditation room, slim and blonde with perfect skin and a soft German accent, wearing a princess-like A-line dress that seemed to twirl even when she was standing still. Deva lived with her young son at the monastery, which she explained was called the 'Place of Stillness'. She did the dark room retreat once a year and found it to be – as she called it – a 'deepening time' and that each person she guided had a different experience in the dark – some were soothed and rested, others confronted deeply repressed parts of themselves. Some experienced joy; others couldn't cope and left early.

When it was time to turn the lights off, Deva came with me to the room, where we sat on the floor, lit a single tealight candle and, in the flickering shadows, she sang a mantra in what I thought must be Sanskrit, her voice clear and steady like a crystal bowl. Then she blew out the flame, and I listened as she stood, her dress swooshing, and left the room.

I was alone in the dark.

The human eye is a remarkable device designed for many eventualities. It can see very well in bright daylight and less so in the dark, but even then, it still works rather well – a fact we often forget in the age of street lights, lamps, LEDs, traffic signals, mood lighting and pathways lit by little twinkling bulbs.

Humans can see in the dark. It's just that we rarely do.

All of the light waves in the universe exist on a spectrum, which ranges from the tightly wound, dark X- and gamma rays on one end to the long, spread-out light of radio and microwaves on the other. A tiny portion in the middle of the spectrum represents the small rainbow of light that human eyes can see. Violet and blue light are more tightly packed with shorter wavelengths that penetrate quickly, while light on the red end comes in longer wavelengths that are slower and easier for the eye to process. This is why we develop 35mm film in a red-lit darkroom and why the blue-white light of an LED street lamp or smartphone will keep you awake at night.

It takes a minimum of twenty minutes for your eyes to adjust to darkness after exposure to light on the blue end of the spectrum. During that time, the pupil opens, or dilates, much like the aperture on a camera, allowing in fainter light from farther away. Shine a bright, blue light into your eye and the pupil quickly closes to prevent the interior parts of the eye from being damaged. Stand outside in the dark and you will be amazed at how much more night-sky detail becomes visible the longer you wait.

In the dark room, though, there is no light whatsoever. The pupil dilates in vain, and the brain works overtime to fill the void, oftentimes creating elaborate visions or blasts of light and colour where there are none. What we see is ultimately an illusion created as the brain attempts to interpret signals sent by the eye.

None of us sees the world exactly the same way.

When I awoke, disoriented, on the first morning, I sat up and stretched, feeling around to remind myself about the size and shape of the bed, then let my feet drop to the floor where they met the scratchy fibres of the oriental carpet. My hands reached out for the side table next to the bed, where I'd placed a few important items – daily medications organised into plastic pill boxes, chapstick, water bottle, lavender hand lotion and a small, embroidered bag containing objects of spiritual and emotional importance to me. There was a piece of rose quartz I often held when I said gratitude mantras; black obsidian that came from my family's land in New Mexico – said to be good for clearing ancient traumas; a piece of smooth Himalayan marble I'd collected the night I spent at Qomolangma; a pendant of Guanyin, the Chinese goddess of compassion; and a sandalwood mala, or string of Tibetan Buddhist prayer beads. It was an assortment of items and traditions that somehow represented a decade of journeys and the unique path that had led me to the dark room.

I sat on the bed for a few minutes, listening for the distant, muffled sounds of movement elsewhere in the building, and wondering if my eyes would adjust and I would start to see outlines and shadows. They didn't. I closed and opened them again – it was the same blackness either way. Then, somewhere upstairs, faraway footsteps.

And the faintest smell of coffee brewing. I figured it must be morning, though I had no idea what time it was nor how long I'd slept.

I got up, moving awkwardly. I found my way to the interior door, then into the antechamber, where I passed the small table on which my meals were to be delivered, and finally the bathroom. My hands felt for the door frames; my leg found the side of the toilet; my hand grasped the cool sink basin and the toothbrush and paste I'd placed along the vanity. Everything needed its spot so I would be able to find it again the next time. Brushing was an act of faith, as I spat into what I hoped was the sink and washed it down with the water that I could hear and feel rushing out of the tap.

As I was drying my hands, I was startled by a knock at the main door, which echoed loudly across the bathroom tiles. My first meal! I rushed back into the main room, stubbing my toe hard on the antechamber food table, closed the inner door and knocked back. I was in extreme pain and grabbed my foot, trying not to curse or cry while I listened for the food delivery – the rustling of a staff member placing a tray, silverware gently clattering, and their soft movement out again. Then the door clicked closed, another knock and I was alone again.

I sat down on the floor for a moment and let tears fall hot and fat while I rubbed my throbbing toe. Why had I rushed? It wasn't like the staff member would have left without feeding me. I made a mental note not to hurry next time and to never rush anywhere in the room again.

Movements had to be slow and deliberate or there would be consequences.

The first meal was heavenly. By feeling around on the tray, I discovered a hard plastic pot containing the main dish, as well as a flask of what smelled like chamomile tea and a mug, a banana and a pear, and a bowl of what seemed like dried fruits and seeds, which made my fingers sticky after I stuck them in to feel around.

I brought the large plastic pot and a spoon into the centre of the room and sat cross-legged on the carpet, remembering a piece of advice I'd read from someone on the internet about their dark room experience: put the silverware in your pocket or you might set it down and never find it again.

Opening the lid, the sweet scent of fruit and cinnamon filled my nose. The spoon was hard to use – it had to be pushed around to gather what felt like a suitable amount, then lifted gingerly to my mouth, delivering porridge with large clumps of what I determined to be fresh peach and pear. I had never tasted fruit so flavourful. The cinnamon burst onto my taste buds. The pear was the sweetest pear I'd ever had. The porridge was warm, soft and comforting. The whole experience was elating, and without being able to see what was in the bowl, I ate with reckless abandon, shovelling the food in gleefully, only hoping not to spill any on myself or the carpet.

I wondered how the meal could be so extraordinarily tasty, and decided that as thoughtful as the monastery's food procurement might be, it had to be an effect of a heightened sense of taste in place of lost sight, rather than some miraculous German farming.

After breakfast, I spent some time – how long I wasn't sure – simply resting, either lying on the bed or sitting on the chair staring into the dark. I did some inner child and inner teenager meditations, accessing early memories and feelings and allowing them to come and be seen as they needed. I may have taken a little nap, but for long periods, especially during the meditations, the difference between sleeping and waking felt sort of fluid.

During a more awake period, I did some yoga on a mat that I'd been given, rolling it out and feeling around for the edges of the carpet and spreading my arms out to make sure I had enough space to move. I ate another pear. I lay flat on the floor for a while because my back had begun to hurt.

Deva came partway through the day, knocking to alert me and then we sat on the floor and listened to each other's voices like ghosts through the blackness. She spoke about trusting the process: not worrying too much about what I would write, trusting that later the words would come. And trusting our bodies, which she said in day-to-day life could sometimes become an 'emotional trash can' and that perhaps the pain in my back was alerting me to some emotions that needed to come out. But I wasn't experiencing as many emotions as I had been expecting to and Deva said she thought our emotions come from outside stimuli. Like light pollution, she said, many things in the outside world can leave you with an impression, and maybe it's those impressions that cause the emotional responses. I wasn't sure, and I needed more time to know what the dark would reveal.

The monastery delivered two meals a day to dark retreatants, so there were no lunches. I came prepared with an excessive amount of comfort snacks that I'm sure the monastery's more devout participants would have thought completely inappropriate: Rice Krispy Treats, croissants, chocolate, tortilla chips, cheesy bread rolls and some spicy German peitschen, which loosely translated as salami 'pork whips', that I'd picked up at the supermarket in Hamburg's train station. Apart from me sneaking in the meat whips, everything at the monastery was completely vegetarian.

Showering in the dark was another adventure, but I found it quite enjoyable. Before the lights went off, I'd checked out the bathroom thoroughly and made a plan. The shower stall was a curtained corner with a floor drain, so there was no basin or lip to step into, and it operated on a simple lever for water and temperature. I undressed completely next to the bed, immediately placed my dirty clothes into a special bag hung off one bedpost, and left a fresh set on the bed. Once I'd felt my way into the bathroom (without stubbing my toe this time) and turned the shower on, the sensation of the water was both exciting and comforting, and I turned it up very hot and let it sprinkle down over my head, noticing properly for the first time in my life how it felt as it dripped off my eyelashes and fingertips. The shampoo and conditioner bottles were another matter – both were the same shape and size and smelled mostly the same, and it was surprisingly difficult to tell them apart with my hands even though I knew they were completely different consistencies. I poured shampoo into one hand and rubbed it all over my head only to find it did not lather and was in fact conditioner, and had to wash everything out and start again.

Dinner was a tagine with tofu, vegetables and couscous, which I once again ate from the plastic pot sitting cross-legged in the middle of the floor and washed down with another flask of chamomile tea. Pouring the tea into the mug required keeping one finger in the mug and pouring with the flask resting against the rim to avoid it spilling over. This also resulted in a burned fingertip each time. I sipped and stared into the dark and felt my muscles relax from the hot shower, and eventually decided the day was most likely over and I could get into bed.

Though I rarely share the extent of my spiritual practice or beliefs with other people, here in the dark it felt entirely freeing to let go and dive as deeply as I wanted. I planned a bedtime ritual involving all of the stones and items I'd brought with me. First, I placed each of the three stones on all of my chakra points, then used the sandalwood mala to count each of the 108 beads while repeating the Tibetan mantra, 'Om mani padme hum' – a foundational Buddhist phrase believed to hold the essence of compassion. Then I brushed my teeth and got under the covers.

I did not have trouble falling asleep.

During what I assumed was the night, I awoke a couple of times, once out of an eerie dream, where I was in a strange, foreign land, it was raining and there was a steep slope ending in an empty cliff edge. Other people were walking along the bottom edge of this slope, but I had to slide down and was worried about tipping over the edge. Then the scene shifted to another street in an economically depressed place. There was a lot of mud and a window, through which I saw a black drone spying on me. I was trying to hide.

When I woke up the next morning, I could still feel the drone's camera penetrating through the dense blackness, and it made me very paranoid.

Before I went into the room, I had spent some time re-reading the *Dao De Jing,* a Chinese philosophical text written around the fifth to sixth centuries BCE by a philosopher-sage known as Laozi. The text is foundational to Daoism, a philosophical and semi-religious belief system that still holds cultural sway over the modern Chinese worldview. It is one of the earliest texts to mention the concepts of yin and yang and its central theme revolves around the Dao, which loosely translates as 'the road' or 'the way'. More deeply, the Dao is a kind of source energy from which all things emanate. (Filmmaker George Lucas drew on Chinese philosophy, especially the idea of the Dao, when he thought up the mysterious 'Force' in *Star Wars,* an ever-present energy that shapes the series' universe and characters.)

In his introduction to the 1996 edition, *Lao-Tzu's Taoteching,* translator Red Pine called the text a 'vision of what our lives would be like if we were more like the dark, new moon'. Laozi taught that the dark can always become light and contains the potential for growth and long life, while light can only become dark and brings with it decay and death. The Chinese character for 'Dao' is made up of two ideograms: 'head' and 'go', and several scholars have suggested that the 'head' could be a reference to the face of the Moon. Thus, the meaning of Dao as 'road' or 'way' comes from watching the face of the Moon moving across the sky. He also notes that Dao shares a linguistic heritage with words that mean 'moon' in several other languages, including Tibetan, Miao, Egyptian and Sanskrit.

Red Pine goes on to state, 'We call people affected by the moon "lunatics", making clear our disdain for its power. Laozi redirects our vision to this ancient mirror. But instead of pointing to its light, he points to its darkness. Every month the moon effortlessly shows us that something comes from nothing. Laozi asks us to emulate this aspect of the moon – not the full moon, which is destined to wane, but the new [dark] moon, which holds the promise of rebirth.'

The idea of dark as yin – feminine, restful, the nothingness out of which everything grows – and light as yang – masculine, active, the creative life force – is compelling to me. If we take these as an energetic spectrum rather than dualistic genders, they become an interesting lens through which to view modern, Western society. It is one in which rest, thinking, self-reflecting, nurturing and darkness – the more 'feminine' aspects – are devalued. Instead, we are hyperenergetic, focused on creation, activity, movement, productivity and 24/7 lights. It is yang over yin, masculine over feminine, light over dark. Does this all sound a bit like capitalism or patriarchy?

'The dark gives the light a place to shine. The light allows us to see the dark,' wrote Red Pine. 'But too much light blinds. Laozi saw people chasing the light and hastening their own destruction. He encouraged them to choose the dark instead of the light, less instead of more, weakness instead of strength, inaction instead of action.'

Try to do nothing. Don't move. Don't read. Don't watch TV or scroll through reels. Don't get up and clean. Don't make a to-do list in your head. Actually, don't think at all. This is what the dark room demands.

There is nothing. No light, no distraction. It is more than an exercise in blindness – though it is that, of course – since blind people might have the luxury of movement, of hearing, of going outside with all their senses.

No, the room wants complete stillness.

By day three, I was in pure agony and hated the room. The muscles in my back had seized up and I was in pain in every position. My mind battled with the request for rest. Instead, I fell back on forty-three years of social programming: the brain processing, trying to change, fix, solve. I asked my body to show me why this pain had come and how to resolve it. Was it all the flying I'd done recently? Was it the new bed, the lack of movement in the room? Let's try some yoga and stretching. Was I carrying some unresolved emotion like Deva said? Nothing came, just muscle spasms.

Please, just show me what I need to do to fix it, I begged my body. She was silent.

You're in pain and you have to stay with it, I heard from somewhere. *The reason doesn't matter; just accept it. That is your lesson.*

I lay flat on the carpet, arms and legs splayed like a starfish, and cried. I couldn't heave or sob or gulp. The tears just flowed cleanly and silently down the sides of my face without effort. I hated the room so much. How could I even think of writing a book about darkness? I bargained with myself: *You could get up and leave. The door is not locked. There are light and movement and people just inches away. You can go.*

Deva came later and suggested I continue trying to stretch and move gently when I was awake. It made me angry that she didn't coddle me or tell me how special I was for doing this really hard thing, and after she left I pounded my fists on the floor and tried to get upset, and that hurt, too. I hated, hated, hated the room.

Lie down, stop, rest. Quiet and consistent. It was the dark's only instruction.

Doing nothing is as vilified as darkness in modern society; it is considered lazy or immoral. Though I am privileged now to live in a culture where days off and sick leave are statutorily guaranteed, I grew up in the United States, perhaps the world's most insane experiment in capitalistic productivity. A place where, if you dare take a day off, never mind a short vacation, you may come back to find your job has been filled by someone else. And you need that job, of course, because without universal healthcare, your job's medical insurance is your only access to a doctor or hospital should the worst happen. And then you regularly need a doctor because your body is broken from working too much without rest.

I've learned as a professional writer that dossing and inertia are crucial parts of my creative process. Ideas are like seeds. They need time to percolate, form and grow up out of the soul before they can be captured on paper. My key to unlocking writer's block is most often to close the laptop and go for a walk in nature or just stop and gaze out into the sky. Some of my best sentences have formed themselves while I was staring blankly at cloud formations. For me, writing works best when I don't try, but instead let ideas flow like a garden hose. You're the vessel for some universal creative energy. Use the Force.

In the twenty-first century, the 'art of yin' has almost become an act of protest, where taking time for yourself to simply experience being alive is something revolutionary. A Google search for books about rest yields dozens of titles like *Rest is Resistance, Radical Rest, Why You Get More Done When You Work Less* and *The Ruthless Elimination of Hurry.*

Productivity is the foundation of our entire society. Let's not forget that some of the first artificial lights were installed in factories during the Industrial Revolution so that, for the first time in human history, line workers could be productive at night, during the hours that nature dictated we should be resting.

By the end of that third day, I realised that *this was it*. The dark room was not about anything at all; it was for sitting, accepting, allowing. I had gone in with an expectation that there would be some type of *experience* in the dark. That I would see visions or gain some profound wisdom. That I would be forced to do deep soul-searching, endure traumatic triggers or face some extreme parts of myself that I'd never reached before. As it turned out, there was only acceptance. Just being there, with no purpose, no revelation, no arcing storyline. Being in the dark was simply the act of being alive, nothing more.

The back pain subsided as I stopped trying to make the room into anything. I stared for long periods of time. I ate more of my snacks and tried using the scented markers I'd bought to draw a picture. I couldn't tell any of the colours apart – they all just smelled artificial, but I made guesses and wrote down what colours I thought I was using. Dinner arrived quicker than I expected, and I realised hours had passed with no trouble at all. The pain wasn't gone, but it was receding.

Look how far you've come now, I told myself as I went

through my now-normalised shower routine. *Only two more meals in here.* And then I almost, *almost*, felt a little pang of nostalgia. I was almost done with the dark room.

I awoke for the toilet and opened my eyes to see, as bright as day, a framed window in front of me, and through it, the cosmos – a stunning and violent swirl of purple gas and starlight. *I must be asleep; it must be a dream*, I thought. Only it wasn't. I blinked. It was still there. I pinched my arm – I was not asleep. I kept watching the gas as it undulated through violet, then a little pink, and thousands of stars shone through the frame.

The final day was relaxed. I allowed myself to go fully into my imagination, lying for hours on the floor letting my thoughts run away into fictional storylines that gave me joy. I was walking in the ancient forests of England that had saved me in the worst times. I was accompanying a beautiful Chilean-American actor to the Oscars in a gorgeous gown. I was exploring the Moon in a rover. I was the size of a tiny particle. I was in Japan – my next destination after the dark room – lazing on a beach, eating noodles and looking at the stars.

With my mind less blocked by expectations, I found access to a lot of stuff stored somewhere in my brain's back rooms. Silly memories came – I was in a tent in the English Lake District with my three girlfriends – GG, Louise and Lauren – in the pouring rain and we were dying of laughter because I had just farted loudly. I was in hysterics with a man I never stopped loving over a video of an Egyptian news anchor and his guest throwing shoes and chairs at each other. Long-lost in-jokes, anecdotes, songs. At least an hour singing Flight of the Conchords, 'Too many dicks on the dance floor, too many dicks on the dance floor, too many dicks.' Asking why just made me laugh more.

I now loved the room because I stopped making it a big deal. I let it be what it was – just a room, without visuals. Or . . . well, nearly.

Apart from the vision of the cosmos, my eyesight had been almost entirely dark, but there were small bursts of colour static, like fireworks or undulating aurora, similar to what you might see if you closed your eyes normally. By the final day in the room, these had evolved into elaborate and sometimes disturbing textures, ranging from a sea anemone, to what I called 'little blub-blubs', loads of barnacles stuck to a rock, and very fine hairs or tendrils. Sometimes there were lots of little stones or warts all bubbled up on a surface, and sometimes what looked like teeth or stalactites, sharp and spiky. These usually moved in a falling cascade with trails after them. Though describing them now they sound horrific, these did not feel disturbing or scary – it was more a sense of wonder as I watched these visions fully open-eyed. The brain trying to make sense of what wasn't there, creating its own light out of the darkness.

We don't often think about how interconnected our senses are. Sight, hearing, taste and smell are all intermixed in the neural system and the brain. Smell and taste are both experienced through the oropharynx, a cavity at the back of the nose and mouth, making them almost interchangeable. Hearing and sight are intimately connected through the vestibulo-ocular apparatus in the inner ear. When you move your head, this apparatus sends signals to your brain about your direction and speed. In turn, the brain signals your eye muscles to move your head and focus your eyes. Changes or problems in the vestibular system result in sensations of dizziness and imbalance.

Without eyesight, the brain relies on other proprioceptors to balance – sensors in our muscles, tendons and joints. My body had adjusted almost immediately to the dark room using my sense of touch, finding walls, furnishings and objects to gain a perception of up and down and find my way. Apart from stubbing my toe in a rush on the first day, it was straightforward to move through the dark using my hands, fingers, shoulders and legs as sensors, and my brain easily stored information about the distances of the different objects in the room. I couldn't see, but my brain filled in the details, giving me a picture in my head of exactly where everything was in the room. So long as I didn't move or change anything, I knew exactly where I was and how to get around.

The final morning arrived. I had no idea what time it was when Deva knocked at the door, not for a check-in but this time to bring me back into the light. She sat down on the

floor, and we spoke for several minutes in the dark, processing my experiences and explaining what would happen
next. She asked me to put the palms of my hands over my
eyes while she lit the same candle we'd blown out four days
earlier.

I shut my eyelids tight and jammed the heels of my hands
into the sockets, grasping at the last seconds of darkness. I
heard the chuck and click of a lighter. The tiny flame blazed
through my bones, skin and eyelids like a supernova. I could
feel the light in the cells of my arms, in my fingertips, in
my hair, and I could see it.

'Take your time,' said Deva, 'Just open your eyes very
very slowly. There's no rush.' I worked my way up to
moving my hands slightly, so more light poured through
the skin of my eyelids. I felt sick and elated at the same time,
like I was flying through a wormhole with no return. After
about fifteen minutes of slowly unclenching, I was able to
gently open the lids of my eyes and felt a rush of dizziness.
Deva recommended lying in child's pose with my knees
tucked and my head on the floor. 'It's grounding for your
balance,' she said.

I put my face to the floor and cried sloppy tears into the
carpet and Deva moved over to unlock the window blinds
and let in some fresh air. 'Just stay there as long as you need
to,' she said over and over. I kept my eyes jammed shut and
my face to the floor, but felt a cool, fresh breeze on my arms
and ears as the window opened.

This must be what it's like to be born.

After about half an hour, I was able to sit up but felt woozy and nauseated — an effect of the inner ear readjusting its balance with the recovered eyesight. I thought I might throw up, so I moved to sit in the chair next to the window. Outside, it was mid-morning, and the birds were loudly chirping in a tree whose leaves were a shade of neon green I was sure I'd never seen before. The sky wasn't blue; it was vivid, bombastic cerulean.

By the afternoon, I was able to stand and move around. Deva had left me to recover privately and suggested a walk outside when I felt able. That was the last time I saw her.

I went out to the shared kitchen area and poured a cup of tea, passing other serene-faced retreatants who had no idea I had just been reborn. I felt ill at ease around the strangers and made my way carefully up a set of steps to an outdoor patio where I sat for several hours, taking in the colours of potted flowers, grass and sky. I must have looked like a true lunatic — a newborn fresh from the womb re-experiencing all of creation for the first time.

In the evening, I wandered down to a pond near the back of the monastery grounds and watched the sun set in an ombré of tangerine, magenta and lavender. Fish bubbled at the surface of the water, bats swooped out of the tall elms catching mosquitos, and the first stars began to appear overhead in a jewel-coloured sky. A sky that had never really been dark, not dark like I knew it.

As it happened, the day I emerged from the dark room was

two days after the summer solstice. I had unwittingly spent the longest days of sunlight in total darkness. There was a full moon, and it was Matariki, the Māori celebration of the rising of the Pleiades star cluster, marking their new year. I checked Facebook – something I had not thought about once in the room – and saw that Dad, Kathryn and their friends in New Zealand were celebrating.

I had no idea how I would process this experience. Maybe I would never be able to fully capture it, and I wasn't worried about it. I would never again look past the brightness of the world's colours, the cheerful greeting of the birds, or the privilege to see and walk among them. And I knew the dark had given me the ability to simply be, with no agenda, task or need.

I had a new appreciation for the delicate balance of night and day. With it, I was going east. I had to know more about how we – me, the birds and bats, the mosquitos and the trees – all of us, need both the night and the day.

8

LIFE

Japan

I heard about Hoshinoya Taketomi Island, a resort in Japan's first Dark Sky Park, while researching a magazine article. It offered a health-and-wellbeing stay themed around darkness and rest, including stretching under the stars, trying local health foods and lying in a float pool under the night sky. I knew I had to go, and told my editor and friends that a trip to Japan would enable me to research how light and dark affect the health of all life forms. But really, this was a gift to myself.

The dark room had taught me that not everything requires a purpose. Did I *need* to go to a tropical resort in Japan? No. I could have researched health and wellbeing in other ways. But given the opportunity, who wouldn't want to spend time on a dark and starry tropical island in Okinawa? I did not take this privilege lightly, while also feeling sad and angry that rest, relaxation and pure sleep in darkness should be a luxury, rather than something available to all.

The dark room also made me hyper-aware of the concept of time, a human construct in many ways, but informed by Earth's natural periods of sunlight and darkness. All living things have evolved to its rhythms over millions of years. The human body has its internal twenty-four-hour clock called the circadian rhythm, which controls several of our behavioural and physical processes. Plants, animals and other types of life have developed similar systems: sunflowers lift their faces toward the rising sun and track it across the sky each day; trees lose their leaves based on the shortening hours of daylight every autumn; birds, butterflies and dung beetles use the movement of the stars to navigate; coral reefs spawn according to the Moon's cycles; and at night, plants produce a hormone called auxin that metabolises energy to grow roots and flower. Nearly every species has some biological system dependent on the natural cycle of night and day.

Emerging from the dark room, I felt I would never again take the rise and fall of daylight for granted, and that first evening on a Japanese beach, watching the sun set a burning orange across the Okinawan island, I felt a little bit like a plant, having stretched my limbs to the daylight, now ready to take root and flower.

In September 2021, a volunteer at the New York Audubon Society found more than 200 dead birds on pavements in

Lower Manhattan around the 3 and 4 World Trade Center skyscrapers, which replaced the buildings destroyed in the September 11, 2001 attacks. A combination of stormy weather and artificial lighting caused the mass death. Though it was not the first nor the last, it received attention when the volunteer, Melissa Breyer, tweeted photos of the deceased birds as she catalogued them.

Not long before, *New York Times Magazine* had published a feature proclaiming, 'The Insect Apocalypse Is Here'. It detailed the worries and research of entomologists world-wide who had begun to think that insect species were disappearing en masse, which the article called 'a loss of abundance that could alter the planet in unknowable ways'. Numerous scholarly papers, popular articles and books have attempted to unpack the complex issue of the mass drop in insect numbers, drawing firm correlations between insect decline and the rise of urbanisation, and specifically calling out light pollution's role in the dwindling numbers of noc-turnal pollinators, such as the often-misunderstood moth.

I began to dig into these correlations and, the more I read, the more worried I became. In his book *Silent Earth*, ecologist Dave Goulson explains that more than 60 per cent of invertebrates – insects, arachnids and shellfish – are nocturnal and most use the light of the Moon for naviga-tion. Moths, for example, fly at a fixed angle to the Moon, gently adjusting their direction as the night progresses and the Moon moves across the sky. They mistake outdoor lights for the Moon, which is how they end up 'trapped' and flittering around lightbulbs and, as Goulson puts it, 'bashing themselves against the light, becoming burned or damaged, exhausting themselves'. A moth can rarely escape once captured in this endless light-circling, and most die of exhaustion.

Moths were a creature I'd rarely thought much about, so I signed up for an expedition with one of England's foremost moth specialists, Matthew Deans. He explained that moth populations have declined by 33 per cent in the last fifty years, threatening plants and the food web, as moths are responsible for pollinating a third of all crops, flowers and trees. Though the bee has become the beloved poster child for pollinator conservation, studies have shown that moths visit different food sources. Bees are drawn to certain crops like cabbage, maple trees and brambles, while moths pollinate nightshades like tomatoes and potatoes, as well as redcurrants, strawberries and stone-fruit trees.

We met at a farm in Suffolk, and Matthew set up traps using black lights, which emit the ultraviolet light that moths are most drawn to. Waking before sunrise, we carefully catalogued the different types that had flown into the traps, then set them free unharmed. This crucial conservation practice allows scientists to track populations and migrations over time. Matthew enthusiastically listed at least 100 different species in our small traps and showed me how fascinating and diverse these creatures are. There was an electric-green brimstone moth with wisps of brown on its delicate wings – these are common in hedgerows and gardens across England; a blood-vein moth, named for the garnet lines of tissue across its wing span; and a giant, fuzzy hawkmoth that had migrated from mainland Europe.

Beyond pollination, nocturnal insects provide many eco-system services – activities that keep Earth's environment functioning. Crickets, for example, are crucial for nutrient recycling and soil regeneration, and fireflies are beautiful and serve as important pollinators, and their larvae feed on snails, slugs and earthworms, which keeps the ecosystem in a delicate balance. Fireflies use their light to communicate and attract a mate. Artificial light at night disrupts this mag-ical courtship ritual, putting nature's living twinkle lights at risk of disappearing completely.

And then there were the bird deaths.

Before going to Japan, I arranged an evening hike with British ornithologist Richard Baines. We met at a pub on the edge of the North York Moors Dark Sky Reserve, and he guided me along a deserted forestry track, where he shouldered a large spotting scope before setting off down a footpath through the trees.

'The first thing you have to know about bird spotting is that you are not going to *see* many birds. You are mostly going to *hear* birds,' he said, raising a shushing finger and whispering the different chirps and calls of several species we could hear in the trees nearby. I closed my eyes, remem-bering how resplendent the birdsong had sounded the day I emerged from the dark room. It was just as lyrical now.

As we walked, Richard explained that ornithologists

have long understood how migratory birds use celestial cues, essentially the light of the stars, for wayfinding. But more recently, they discovered an additional mechanism – a special molecule that makes birds' eyes magnetic, creating a visual compass that helps them navigate using the Earth's magnetic field. He said that light pollution interrupts all of these visual processes, sending birds off course, disturbing migration patterns and causing the mass deaths I'd read about, as birds become dazzled and confused by high-rise lighting and consequently fly toward cities and into tall buildings. A 2024 study published in the journal *PLoS One* revealed the startling figure that, in the US alone, more than a billion birds die from building collisions every year.

Lighting controls proved to be crucial to the care and breeding success of Arctic birds at the North Carolina Zoo and Aquarium. The facility uses heavily controlled lighting that mimics the natural lengths of day and night in the far northerly latitudes where its resident murres (guillemots), auklets and puffins originate. The lighting controls have ensured the birds moult, mate and even migrate within their zoo habitats. And birds aren't the only species affected by light pollution. Plants also have photoreceptors, which essentially allow them to 'see' and photosynthesise light into energy for their growth. These receptors also help them know when to grow, flower and shed their leaves for the winter. Trees have been proven to bud earlier in the spring and lose their leaves later into the autumn or winter if they live near bright street lights, as their receptors cannot tell the difference between artificial light and daylight.

As the pink Yorkshire evening settled over the forest, we came to a clearing where Richard stopped and nodded to indicate the dreamy hoots of tawny owls calling to each other through the branches.

'Owls wake up around this time after the sun has set and they hoot for a variety of reasons. These two are probably males calling to establish their territory. There may be a female nearby they are trying to impress,' he said.

Just then, a brown bird swooped over us and Richard gasped – a woodcock! 'This is incredible, they are very shy birds! Getting a sighting like this is so rare,' he said, explaining that the elusive nocturnal birds have long, tapering bills that they use to hunt through the soil for worms.

'They hide in the undergrowth during the day, so you have to be out in the evening to see them.' We stood and watched, silent and wide-eyed, as the bird continued to soar up and down over the clearing and then eventually disappeared into the night.

The day before my flight to Tokyo, I spent a while looking over the map of East Asia. Japan stretches alongside Russia down below the Korean peninsula, and if you zoom in, hundreds more of its small islands sweep far to the south. It's a deceptively large country, and my fiery sunset beach was on a tiny island at its very southern reaches. Part of Okinawa

Prefecture in a small archipelago called the Yaeyama Islands, Taketomi is nearly 2,000 kilometres from the Japanese capital – a 2.5-hour flight south over increasingly turquoise water where the East China Sea joins the mighty expanse of the Pacific Ocean.

At just five and a half square kilometres, Taketomi is a culture unto itself, with unique traditions, beliefs, foods and a dialect spoken by families indigenous to the island. It is a stub of ancient coral reef rising out of the sea with a resident population of around 350 people, who live in one low-rise, traditional village. There are a lot of day visitors who take the ferry over from larger Ishigaki Island, which has the airport where I arrived from Tokyo. But overnight visitors are rare on little Taketomi and there is only one place to stay: the Hoshinoya hotel.

As a general rule, I don't like it when resorts open in small communities or areas where the ecosystem is delicate. In my years of travel journalism, I've observed that it rarely goes well and can end up with corporations polluting the environment and exploiting the community. So I wasn't sure what to expect when I got to Taketomi, but I was pleasantly surprised.

Hoshinoya is owned by Hoshino Resorts, a Japanese heritage brand that started its first hot-spring resort on Honshu, Japan's main island, in 1914, catering to liberals, artists, authors and poets in the Roaring Twenties. The company's history is one of eco-consciousness, from its early adoption of hydroelectric power in 1929 to helping end the formerly popular Japanese practice of eating wild birds and establishing one of Japan's first bird sanctuaries in the 1970s.

I was greeted at the ferry port by Yuki Kuramochi, the hotel's PR manager — a kind-faced woman in her twenties who spoke soft English and took me on a tour of the grounds, explaining that Hoshinoya did extensive community consultations before opening the property and took great care with its environmental specifications, down to designing the layout of the resort around several ancient mangrove trees so as not to disturb them.

'The architects actually lived in the community and were fully integrated with the locals for months beforehand,' Yuki said, walking me through the island's main village at sunset. 'You can see here, the houses are all one storey with red tile roofs and are surrounded by coral-stone dry walls, which are called gukku; they protect the homes from typhoons and our local south winds.'

As the entire island is an architectural preservation area, the resort constructed each guest room as a villa in the style of a traditional village home. They also employed a specialist lighting firm to create a low-lit, well-shielded and warm-tone lighting scheme that adhered to the requirements of the Dark Sky Park, with the aim of protecting the island's delicate nocturnal ecosystem and starry skies.

We strolled along a dirt track away from the main cluster of village homes to meet up with stargazing guide Maoko Ishihara, who led us up a small hill to a rock formation with a perfectly round hole.

'This rock is called Hoshimi Ishi, explained Maoko. 'Hoshi means star in Japanese, mi means watching, and ishi means stone. So, this is the Star-Watching Stone.'

Since ancient times, the villagers have used the stone to check for the changing of the seasons – the harvest was signalled when a star cluster called Subaru was visible through the hole.

'Subaru is very famous in Japan,' she said. 'It is a group of six stars together. We also have a car company with this name, and its logo has six stars.'

I had to laugh. Here it was again, our old pal: Subaru was the Japanese name for the Pleiades, the same star cluster I'd been introduced to in New Zealand as Matariki and in Ladakh as Min-duk, and the one the Native American Diné people referred to as Sparkling Seeds. It seemed that every culture had developed a special connection to the same group of stars that my sister and I loved as kids, including villagers on a tiny island in the Pacific Ocean.

I excitedly told Yuki and Maoko what I had learned.

'That's amazing!' exclaimed Maoko. 'We thought those stars were only famous here!'

The central cluster of the Pleiades is around 8 light years away, but some of the stars are up to 43 light years away. With the naked eye, somewhere between six and fourteen stars are visible, depending on factors such as your elevation, how clear the air is and your eyesight. This accounts for the varied naming conventions, usually relating to the six or seven brightest stars that are most easily seen. But look through a telescope and around a thousand stars can come into view.

As the night drew in, we wandered on from the Star-Watching Stone and let our eyes adjust to the dark, not turning on torches, our feet finding their way along the bumps in the track. Maoko told me that she recently completed an astronomy guiding certification offered by the prefectural government, so she could create tours and have new opportunities with the resort.

'The stargazing activities have been very popular with our guests,' she said. 'Most of the people who stay overnight here are specifically coming for dark skies.'

At the bottom of the road, we reached a pier where people had gathered to see the night sky. The last ferry back to Ishigaki had long since departed with all the day trippers. But the locals go down to the pier most evenings in clear weather to watch the sunset and hang out by the water. We stood on the pier for a while, drinking woody, cold oolong tea from flasks that Yuki had packed and talking about the island and the sky. Maoko pointed out a pair of bright stars just above the southern horizon, hanging so low that they cast two long reflections stretching like lighthouses across the calm seawater.

'Those are the top part of the Southern Cross,' she said, explaining how the whole constellation is only visible from the Southern Hemisphere, but Taketomi is close enough to the equator that its top stars are just barely visible along the horizon.

It was nearing 10 p.m. by the time I got back to my room. The ankle-height path lights gave a warm glow the colour of firelight, just enough to see my way, while the Milky Way spread like a thin, bright cloud across the sky. Inside, I checked my blood pressure – a nightly ritual, having inherited the family tradition of hypertension. It was at 116/72 – the lowest in a long time. I shut myself into the bedroom, sliding closed the shoji, a traditional Japanese room divider, and cuddled into the bed – a thick mattress on the floor. The room was perfectly dark, and, for a moment, I felt like I was back in the dark room. It was comforting, and I slept soundly without waking.

In 2016, the American Medical Association (AMA) released a groundbreaking report linking the then-new light-emitting diodes (LEDs) – a semiconductor lighting technology heralded as being more energy-efficient and cost-friendly – with a slew of human health problems. The report detailed scientific evidence that exposure to blue-spectrum white light at night, such as that produced by LEDs, correlated with increased risks for cancer, diabetes and heart disease.

Doctors had known for a while by then that blue-rich light at night, such as the light from phones, laptops and TVs, was problematic for our circadian rhythm. The body uses a decrease in daylight as its cue to release a hormone called melatonin, which is responsible for sending our nervous system into 'rest and digest' mode and putting us to sleep. Consuming too much light at night, especially blue-spectrum light, can and does disrupt our sleep cycles, resulting in mental health issues and depression.

The 2016 publication showed that knock-on effects ranged throughout the body. More research was conducted in the intervening years, including a 2017 Harvard study which found that women who live in areas with higher levels of outdoor light at night, especially night-shift workers, may be at higher risk for breast cancer. Then, in early 2024, a study published in the journal *Environmental Pollution* showed that exposure to nighttime light was associated with a 21 per cent higher risk of cardiometabolic diseases, including heart attack, stroke, diabetes, insulin resistance and heart failure.

Despite my involvement in advocacy against light pollution, I had never really stopped to consider whether it might be affecting my own body physically.

In 2023, when I was only forty-one years old, I had a sudden heart attack and subsequently underwent angioplasty, an operation where a small piece of wire mesh was inserted into my artery to open the blockage and keep blood flowing to my heart. I was awake during the surgery, and although it is a very common procedure and was performed by the best surgeons, I could feel everything, and it was mentally traumatising. It took months to heal physically, and among the instructions for heart rehab was to make sure I reduced my stress levels and got plenty of quality, uninterrupted sleep.

Understanding what causes any given health problem is sometimes an impossible task – a confusing mix of genetics, family history, lifestyle choices, childhood traumas, psychological conditions, education, socioeconomics and physical surroundings can all contribute. I knew I had not won the genetic lottery, having cardiovascular disease and high blood pressure on one side of my family and high cholesterol on the other. But after the heart attack, I became acutely aware of anything that might raise my blood pressure or put stress on my heart.

When the 2024 study came out a year after the attack, I spent sleepless nights under the London street lamp that glowed into my bedroom and wondered what sinister things the city lights might be doing to me. For all of the benefits of living in a metropolis, and there are many – incredible food, an amazing community and friend group, access to the greatest cultural institutions, not to mention the location for my work as a travel journalist – I felt ill at ease and began to wonder if I should leave London altogether, for my heart's sake. It wasn't something I *wanted* to do, but I could manage it if I needed to.

But I was just one of millions of people affected by high stress levels and poor sleep, to which the city's glaring, all-night lights contribute. I could potentially afford to leave, but many people could not, and what about them? Don't we all deserve access to a night that keeps our circadian rhythms ticking?

*

I awoke the next morning in my Japanese futon bed, rested and relaxed. Yuki came in a golf cart and took me to the island's town hall, which also housed a museum, library and tourist information centre wrapped into one. The morning was already hot and I had tropical-humidity sweat pouring from my forehead but, once inside, the cooling effects of the traditional Taketomi architecture were immediate. Constructed of wooden beams and the signature red-tile roof, the building was left open to the air on its southeast side, letting in a pleasant, warm breeze that circulated through the room while I looked at displays and books chronicling the island's ecosystem, plants, animals and stories, many of which had only recently been written down. All of it was proof of the Taketomi people's strong connection to their unique little slice of the Earth. They knew the calls of the birds that would signal the rains, how to build naturally cooling homes and which rising stars signalled the harvest.

One display explained that each of the village's three entrances had a Sunmashaa, or sacred place with a tree surrounded by a stone wall built according to the design principles of feng shui. These kept diseases and evils out of the village. It listed beautifully specific words in the local dialect describing the islandscape:

- Pii: the edge on the offing side of the coral reef which dries up at ebb tide;
- Fuchi/Guchi/Mizo: the break of a coral reef;

- Soi: the rock and coral reef projecting on the sea;
- Bata/Yuni: a sand spit;
- Kachi/Gumi: the trick to catch fish left by an ebb tide by enclosing the stone walls as if forming the shape of a horseshoe.

And there were creatures seen on the land and in the sea:

- the Tree Nymph, an elegant black-and-white butterfly whose larvae feed on poison grass;
- the Piiyoo, a brown bird often singing lively [sic] together that loves flower nectar and sweet fruits;
- the Koobui or Ryukyu flying fox, a large bat with round eyes that flies in a pitch-dark night with no ultrasonic waves;
- the Haroo or ghost crab, a nocturnal crab living on the beach with a large square body and pointy, protruding eyes.

A shelf of hand-bound books explained Indigenous cultural traditions and knowledge:

- The Day of Junguya, or Full Moon Festival, when the men of Taketomi Island would take out a hatagashira banner and play tug-of-war;
- if the Piiyoo bird sings, it will rain;
- the distinct hoshizuna, or star sand, is made up of star-shaped particles, the remains of a single-celled

marine organism that washed up on shore at Kaiji Beach on the island's southwest.

The last one caught my eye. The presence of a beach full of star-shaped sand! Yuki promised we'd go see it, but first, I should read the island's constitution, displayed on a brown plaque near the entrance. It proclaimed the people's pride in their traditional culture and natural surroundings inherited from their ancestors and a commitment to working together. Its five community principles were: No Selling, No Pollution, No Disturbance, No Destruction, and Revival.

We will strive to maintain and preserve village landscapes by conforming to the ways of the ancient Ryukyus. We will preserve tranquillity, orderly calmness and good morals. We will strive to gain an understanding of our island's history and culture, enrich our culture and enhance the character of our culture. We will have great respect for traditional festivals, revive indigenous industries, and convey our island spirit. We will make the best use of the unique characteristics of our island and strive to develop and improve island life through the efforts of the local islanders.

It was the simplest and most enlightened constitution I'd ever heard of.

After that, Yuki drove me down to Kaiji Beach, so I could see the star sand. Not really sand, the grains are the exoskeletons of tiny, single-celled organisms called *Baculogypsina*. Once a living organism in the Pacific Ocean, when the *Baculogypsina* die, their millimetre-sized shells stay in the sea until the tide washes them ashore. We met a man at a small hut selling tiny glass vials of star sand and paper-weights with a few grains suspended in clear resin. Signs nearby warned tourists not to take the star sand away – the vendor was one of only a few locals authorised to dive for the star sand offshore, where it wouldn't erode the beach. He hand-made all of his products and donated the proceeds to marine conservation and beach clean-up.

The people of Taketomi were deeply connected to their island: a five-square-mile stub of coral reef filled with life-giving plants, surrounded by the rich but delicate sea and prone to storms and winds.

In October 2023, a paper published in the journal *Nature Mental Health* showed findings from the largest-ever study of 86,000-plus participants on nighttime light exposure. Participants wore a triaxial accelerometer on their wrists containing a sensor to measure their light exposure over seven days. Unsurprisingly, the study found that exposure to light at night disrupts circadian rhythms and increases the risk for psychiatric disorders and depression. The paper stated that 'the simple practice of avoiding light at night and seeking brighter light during the day could be an effective, non-pharmacological means of reducing serious mental health issues'. A similar study conducted in Japan in 2022, and published in *Environmental Research*, concluded that participants exposed to more intense light in their bedrooms were significantly associated with obesity, high lipids, systemic inflammation, sleep disturbances and depression.

If exposure to excess light at night harms our health, could natural darkness improve it? It turns out that darkness is good for our minds and spirits, as well as our bodies. In February 2024, a 'Night Sky Connectedness Index' was published in the *Journal of Environmental Psychology*. It showed that a greater connection to the night sky was positively related to a person's mental health and happiness and that experiencing the beauty and wonder of the natural world can evoke positive emotions and a sense of awe. The International Astronomical Union (IAU) recognises the positive wellness effects of the night sky, and that contemplating a starry sky from a dark, natural place elicits a feeling of awe strongly connected with positive emotions and attitudes. People who acknowledge feeling part of a greater entity, whether humanity, nature or a spiritual force, report increased gratitude and empathy.

In his 2023 book *Awe*, psychologist Dacher Keltner wrote about the beneficial effects of awe on our physical, mental and emotional wellbeing. His research showed that experiencing awe can reduce stress, quiet our inner critic and inspire us to act unselfishly toward others. When we spend time in naturally dark environments, we get new ideas, create bolder artistic outputs and experience fresh ways of thinking.

*

By my third day on Taketomi Island, I could feel my body slowing down, not to the inertia of the dark room, but the tension had dropped out of my muscles, my breathing was deep and regular, and the sluggishness I often experienced in London, even after sleeping, was gone. I knew part of it was the long sleeps with no street light, and part was the pace of the trip: everything on Taketomi was quiet and unhurried.

I ate most of my meals in the villa, away from the intense equatorial sunlight and humidity. There were mozuku soba, delicate Okinawan noodles served cold with local seaweed and that same seaweed in pickled form; umibudou or 'sea grapes' – another type of seaweed so named because of its clustered spheres that burst in your mouth; taco rice – an Okinawan speciality created in the 1980s for US soldiers stationed on the prefecture's main island; and the daily breakfast boxes that ranged from fresh fish and clams to soft-tofu porridge and bowls of local grains and fruits.

The noodles, fruits and cereals were easy to gobble down, but some of the dishes were a bit more challenging for me and I did struggle to enjoy fresh clams for breakfast. But I also figured the people of Taketomi had honed this diet over centuries and knew what was best to eat at which times of day and year. I started to feel refreshed, rested and somehow in sync with the whole island.

One evening, I met Yuki and Maoko by the pool, which was a large oval sunk into the middle of the property and surrounded by grass embankments. As we waited for darkness to fall, we admired the design of the pool, which was sparsely landscaped so that it would reflect starlight. We talked about the distances of different stars we could see, and I recalled what I'd learned in Uzbekistan: how the light from the farthest stars is sometimes hundreds or thousands of years old by the time it reaches our eyes.

Then they gave me a floaty noodle and I slipped into the pool, leaning my head back until my hair was soaked in the cool water and my body went limp. The only noise was the sound of crickets chirping and the occasional splash as the only other guest in the pool redirected their floaty somewhere off in the shadows at the other end. I could feel my mind starting to churn, my brain itching to plan for the upcoming trip home and what I would write about all of this. But I had learned from the dark room.

Not now, I told my brain. *Now, we stop and rest.* And that's what we did. Staring at the stars, unthinking, until my fingers wrinkled up and then it was time again to sleep.

On the final night, Yuki took me down to the beach after dinner for a stretching session with the resort's resident wellness practitioner, Merii Okumura. The owls were calling in surround sound from the forest behind the beach and, as it grew darker, fireflies flickered, looking for romance among the lower shrubs.

Merii explained that the resort developed its own unique stretching activity, called Tinnu Shinkoke, which means 'deep breathing of the sky' in the Okinawan dialect. They brought together different traditions, such as tai chi, yoga, Japanese martial arts and meditation, with the goal of feeling connected to the cosmos and gaining self-awareness by focusing on the breath and the sky.

'I've been so busy these days,' said Yuki, 'but these last nights, when I saw the beautiful stars with you, somehow I felt so relaxed. It was like a relief. And the same tonight.'

For a while, we sat in silence on our mats letting the night fall darker and darker around us, the fiery sky fading to blue then black. The beach was quiet except for a local family that Yuki knew – parents and two kids who were watching the sunset, splashing in the darkening water, their laughter floating away to the sea. A few others came and went – a tour guide bringing guests to shore in an old fishing boat, and a stargazing group looking for the different constellations of the zodiac.

Merii cycled us through several types of breathing from the abs and chest combined with gentle movements like arm stretches, twists, shoulder rolls and gentle shaking to help with blood circulation.

At the end, she told us to put our hands to the sky and absorb its power, then place the palms over our eyes, feeling the energy and transferring it from hands to eyes, ears, neck and heart. Finally, we lay down in silence and focused on the sounds we could hear. The island was alive all around.

There were lapping waves.

Crickets. Leaves rustling in a warm breeze. The call of a late-running owl.

The odd splash of a fish in the shallows. The wind drawing my hair against my ears. A foot straying onto sand.

And there was my own breath. In and out; in and out. There was me, alive with my own beating heart.

9

LOVE

Argentina

'Megan. No hablas mucho. ¿Por qué estás tan callado?'

Domingo leaned forward from the back seat and softly asked why I was so quiet. We were alone in the truck. Somewhere outside Posadas, we'd stopped at a petrol station and the others had gone inside for snacks.

'Lo siento.' I tried to blame the reasons for my silence on my poor Spanish, but it wasn't the whole truth. The night before, in the dark, the Guaraní chief had cleansed me with smoke while Ale stood a whisper away and translated. I had been in a cold sweat.

'Domingo says you have a fever.' Ale's voice was low and close in the dark. 'You need to take care of your body while you are still in Argentina.'

Domingo had intuitively known I was in the middle of

a sea change, and it was because of Ale and the night and the Argentinean heat.

Ale – short for Alejandro – had met me a couple of weeks earlier at the Iguazu border, where Argentina splits from Brazil in a flood of waterfalls that spill over every ledge and crevice for miles. I'd got up early to watch the sunrise over the Brazilian side of the falls, then caught a taxi to the border and walked across. Ale greeted me on the busy road outside passport control with a double-cheek kiss, while trucks whizzed by, kicking up dust, and told me it was too hot to do anything except sit in the pool that day.

It was the beginning of February – the dead of summer – and the domo de calor, a high-pressure weather system that frequently traps hot air in the region, had descended over Misiones – the long, narrow finger of a province that juts from northern Argentina towards Paraguay and Brazil. Temperatures were pushing into the high 40s Celsius.

Ale and I were already friendly. I'd interviewed him over Zoom a couple of years previously and written a profile on him as the founder of DarkSky Argentina. I was especially taken by his work with the Guaraní, an Indigenous community that was trying to save their nighttime heritage, which included star stories, sky wisdom and fire rituals. He'd been intimately invited into the community through a Guaraní baptism and received an Indigenous name.

Ale had almost singlehandedly convinced the provincial government to institute a night-sky protection law, which saw its street lights changed for dark-sky-friendly ones. He was also the director of ecotourism for the Misiones tourism ministry, and an astronomer, keen birder and solo dad. When I emailed him to say I wanted to go to Argentina to meet the Guaraní, he wrote back in a single sentence: 'Just tell me when you are coming.'

My intention was to learn about the Guaraní beliefs about fire. From my conversations with Ale, I knew they used fire ceremonies and torches to enter the jungle at night when they believed it was inhabited by bad spirits. People could not enter without a ritual blessing and the protection of bamboo torches called takua recha.

I'd dreamed of going to Argentina for years. When I imagined it, I saw the sharp shale peaks of the Tierra del Fuego, Patagonia's crusted, blue glaciers and windswept tundra, the tango clubs of Buenos Aires, and the Pampas grasslands where gauchos still roamed on horseback. Misiones was nothing like that. It was humid and carpeted in lush, green selva – jungles of South American Atlantic Forest, thick with giant mahogany trees, jacarandas and indigenous pines. Everything grew up out of clayish red soil that covered shoes, cars and homes in a rosy hue, giving the region its nickname as the tierra colorada, or red earth.

Although it makes up only 1 per cent of Argentina's total land area, Misiones holds more than half the country's biodiversity. It is a dense, tropical corridor teeming with beehives, jaguars and rare birdsong.

Indigenous to the region, the Guaraní historically

lived across a large swath of what is now southern Brazil, Paraguay, Argentina and parts of Uruguay. There are many different Guaraní communities and family groups, and they are most often associated with Paraguay, where Guaraní is one of the national languages. In the sixteenth and seventeenth centuries, the Spanish and Portuguese invaded and colonised the region, and many Guaraní were subjected to slavery and Christian conversion by Jesuits, who had established mission churches here. The modern-day province of Misiones was named for those missions.

Ale drove me a few miles from the border to an eco-lodge, where I stowed my rucksack in an A-frame cabin with brick floors and timber ceilings. It was cool inside, a relief from the relentless humidity. He brought a large insulated bottle and set it on the table along with a cup made from a carved-out gourd. It was overflowing with a mound of dry leaves: yerba mate. Mate is considered the national drink of Argentina, but it originated with the Guaraní and, Ale told me, most of the best yerba mate farms were right here in Misiones. He poured hot water from the bottle over the leaves, wetting down only one side. He then stuck a metal straw, called a bombilla, into the drenched side, took a deep swig and offered it to me. Mate is a sharing drink, I learned quickly, as the cup would be passed around in turns for a group to share from the same straw.

The taste was unfamiliar, bitter and nutty, something like a distant cousin of green tea – very distant – and I liked it. We shared the cup back and forth, Ale teaching me the etiquette of mate drinking: never touch the bombilla; always return the cup to the pourer when you've finished your round; only say 'thank you' when you don't want any more – instead say 'Que buen mate' or 'What a good mate' to indicate you like it. Later, he would show me how to be the cebadora, who pours a round for each person in a clockwise direction or sometimes in order of who joined the group first.

We drank a lot of mate together over the next ten days, driving all over Misiones and further, through jungle, town and wetland, me pouring and him behind the wheel of the white pickup truck; both of us talking, talking, talking about everything – the hot weather and climate change, the Argentinean dialect, his son and our vastly different families, Argentina's economic problems, nature, birds, spirituality and the thing that brought us together in the first place: the dark.

Humans have been using fire for hundreds of thousands of years. Possibly even a million years. The fossil record shows traces of ancient ash and charcoal in southern Africa and the Middle East. Humans likely came upon fire by accident in African bushlands ignited by lightning strikes. Early people would've understood its potential for destruction, warmth and light, and probably first began experimenting by opportunistically fuelling natural fires. Before we learned the process of ignition, having fire required keeping existing fires burning – eternal flames that were carried, stoked and transferred hand-to-hand, carefully, across landscapes.

In his book, *Fire: A Brief History*, Stephen J. Pyne called the Earth's naturally ignited fires 'First Fire', while the human-harnessed and controlled fire was 'Second Fire'. 'Once fire bonded with humanity,' he wrote, 'it had also to respond to ideas, institutions, beliefs, trade and taste as much as to winds and ravines.'

He pointed out that deciding to start a fire, quell it or change its rhythms all have biological consequences, killing, remaking or paving the way for life big and small. 'It stirs molecules, organisms, landscapes. It kills plants, breaks down ecological structures, sets molecules adrift, shuffles species, opens up niches, and for a time rewires the flow of energy and nutrients.' Fire can kill plant life, yes, but it can also clear dead brush, making way for new sprouts to emerge.

Just as the biomes of Yellowstone responded when wolves were reintroduced and created new 'landscapes of fear', the presence or absence of even a small fire could change whole ecosystems. And we've been using it so long that no landscape anywhere is left untouched by the influence of human-fanned flames.

For thousands of years we lived with fire as our only reliable source of light at night, natural but artificially made. A protector in the jungle and a saviour in the savannah. A way to prepare meals and keep warm. Also a destroyer of homes and food sources. And a spiritual guide, a god.

LOVE

Over time, we evolved with and by fire, learning to tend it carefully, gingerly, with due respect afforded to its powers to illuminate, to give and to take away. Fire made toxic foods consumable and evolved human anatomy, removing the need for huge muscles in the skull to chew uncooked material. Our lives after dark were lived around the fire. It altered our social relationships as communities emerged: we composed and told stories, our faces lit by its dim flickering. 'The stories that transformed a day's tasks into a moral universe,' Pyne wrote.

Afterwards we stood watch, scared away predators and found our way along darkened tracks with its amber glow, and we made love by its soft warmth.

That first evening, Ale arranged a stargazing session at the eco-lodge. Two other guests, backpackers from France, had signed up. As the sun was setting pink over the cabins, we ventured into the heat on a trail that led into the jungle behind the lodge, through a tangle of vines, banana leaves the size of my torso, and enormous palo de rosa trees that towered over the canopy. Above us, a hubbub of selva birds – toucans, macaws, parrots – were engaged in evening chatter.

In a grassy clearing, wooden benches had been set in a circle around a fire pit. Bamboo torches flickered, their smoke promising to keep the aggressive mosquitos at least partially at bay. The circle of sky above the clearing turned purple and Saturn popped through.

I could understand more Spanish than I could speak, thanks to years of school learning in New Mexico, but the Argentinean accent was a different story. The French back-packers were more fluent, so I agreed that Ale could carry out his presentation in Spanish, even though really I was absorbing very little of what he was saying. His voice was gentle but deep and he spoke fast, with a lilt that seemed to glide effortlessly through consonants and skip over whole syllables. The temperature stayed high. Sweat formed at my temples and skated down my spine. Fire smoke singed my throat. Mosquitos pricked my skin. And, as darkness fell, Ale's stories lulled me into a dreamy haze.

Somewhere outside the clearing, there were strange flashes over the treetops. 'La policía?' the others wondered. There was no rain, but I knew it was not the police. Sparks were flying. It was lightning.

Humans are the only species so far known in the universe that can control and create fire, bending it to our will. The annual walking tracks of Aboriginal Australian communities became 'threads of fire' that followed their songlines – the pathways of knowledge that these communities used to cross the continent. The night sky aided their navigation, so the songlines were intricately interwoven with stories of the stars, the cosmos, the origins of life and the meaning of everything. Where the Aboriginal peoples walked the songlines, they left behind remnants of the fires they lit each night – pockmarks of charcoal that all together drew a charred map of the constellations. It was around these fires each evening that knowledge was shared and stories of the stars passed between generations.

Orion's belt, Matariki, the Diné Sparkling Seeds and Subaru were all shared and learned by a fire. Ulugh Beg wrote down his star catalogue by oil lamp and candlelight. In this way, our knowledge of the stars cannot be separated from the fires that illuminated our nights over the millennia. Firelight was not the enemy of the night sky, quite the opposite: its soft amber light falls in the longer-wavelength red end of the visible spectrum. Perhaps our eyes even evolved this way precisely because of our close relationship with fire.

Controlled fires like torches and campfires could cast just enough glow to illuminate the immediate surroundings without polluting a wider area. Other creatures, particularly predators like wolves and lions, instinctually understood its dangers, thus moving humans to the very centre of the food web. With fire, we became super-predators, taking over the planet like the myths and gods we invented around its flames. Our intelligence evolved through the refined diet it provided, and the knowledge shared around it.

Growing up in a high desert region, fire was part of my life from a young age. In the winter we stoked the wood-stove, which warmed our adobe home with the sweet, piney scent of burning piñon wood and cedar; in autumn everything smelled of unripened green chile peppers being slowly roasted over flames; and in summer the air often grew thick with the smoke of mountain wildfires. These were sometimes the result of lightning strikes, and sometimes human intervention, either controlled burns that raged out of control or, worst of all, a campfire or cigarette butt that lit and razed through dry pine forests in the upper elevations.

New Mexico is so fire-prone that the state is the home of Smokey the Bear, a cartoon bear whose job is a park ranger who warns about the dangers of fire. *Only YOU can prevent forest fires!* he proclaims on signs across the state. The Smokey character was based on a real bear – a 3-month-old black bear cub that was orphaned in a 1950 wildfire in the Capitan Mountains of New Mexico.

One autumn a few years ago, I was back for a visit and took a drive through the northern part of the state, up to the towns of Taos and Angel Fire, following US Highway 64. It is a long road that goes right the way from the New Mexico-Arizona border to Whalebone Junction at Cape Hatteras in North Carolina – the Atlantic, as far east as you can go. I was at the western end, and out there, it's just a tiny, two-lane mountain byway that doesn't feel like it would go anywhere except over remote passes and into Angel Fire and Eagle Nest. These places were the stuff of dreams on the evening weather report when I was a child. They have magical names that seemed even more magical as a kid. They were always forecast to get snow in the winter, and for that, I was constantly wishing to go to them.

The high alpine deserts of southern Colorado and northern New Mexico are home to the Muache, a southern tribe of the Indigenous Ute people, who came to this area specifically to perform autumn ancestral ceremonies to their Great Spirit. They were the first here and the first to notice the evening alpenglow that pulsated in blazing colours around a mountain that later came to be known in Spanish as Agua Fría – Cold Water Peak. The Muache called this glow the 'fire of the gods', and later, in the 1780s, Franciscan friars altered their semantics, poetically giving us Angel Fire. Indeed, it was because of this burning colour that the Spanish called the entire mountain range Sangre de Cristo: the 'blood of Christ'.

As I drove, the road gently switchbacked through pine forest, which had climbed to a height at Palo Flechado Pass a few miles before, and then opened into an expansive, treeless valley surrounded by dark green peaks. Much of the pasture was still covered in snow. There was not a single car heading northeast with me, so I pulled off, rolled down the driver's side window and began snapping pictures of 4,000-metre Wheeler Peak, the state's highest mountain. Though I knew it was treacherous, from that distance it looked tame and seemed almost ordinary compared to the mountains of similar height I saw in Tibet and Ladakh.

From there, the road wound into a devasted landscape of black, charred pine trees and burnt earth. The Ute Park Wildfire had devastated nearly 150 square kilometres earlier that year. Homes gone, animals lost, memories vanished in seconds, minutes, long, singeing days. It takes years for an arid landscape to recover from a forest fire.

How long would I have to wait to drive that road again and see things growing?

'The Guaraní have a unique relationship with time and commitments,' Ale told me as we drove toward the Yvytu Porá community, where he worked closely with Domingo, the community's second chief. We were following an empty, paved highway that reminded me of the road to Angel Fire. Cresting a hill, the jungle spread like a dark green ocean in front of us.

The community lived in the valley down a short dirt drive – a small collection of buildings made of timber, bamboo reeds and mud.

'The men aren't here. Domingo is gone,' one of the residents told Ale. 'They are all watching the football match in the next village.'

'See?' he said as we got back into the truck. 'Domingo might tell you he will be here, but everything is fluid. Time is not a commodity for them.'

We drove instead to the Parque Salto Encantado, a nature park up the road where Ale and Domingo co-presented a regular stargazing event called Cielo Guaraní, or Guaraní Sky. During these events, Ale would first introduce the science of Western astronomy and then Domingo shared Guaraní knowledge of the night sky and stories of the constellations.

The day was hot and the park was almost empty. We walked in silence down a paved pathway, butterflies flitting all around us. At the bottom, the path gave way to a deep gorge and the rumble of a huge waterfall, the Salto Encantado, which was formed by a river called Cuña Pirú. I leaned onto a railing and looked out into the chasm, straining to see the cascade through moss and dripping vines. Ale stood next to me, and I felt the brush of his arm on mine. He said there was a Guaraní legend that the Salto Encantado was born from the tears of a young woman who fell in love with the chief's son of their enemy tribe. She mourned the conflict and felt such deep, unrequited love that strings of water fell from her eyes and the gods turned them into the waterfall.

'They say if you touch the river's water, you will find your one,' he said quietly. I was trying to focus but a cold sweat was rising up my neck and I wasn't sure what to do next. Was I getting feelings for this man who lived 7,000 miles from me? Or was he just putting on a very good Latin-American show? I took out my phone and snapped a selfie, then looked at him, trying to keep hold of his brown eyes.

'Picture?'

I'd ruined the moment, but we took a selfie together. Later, I put the photo on my Instagram story and was flooded with replies from my girlfriends: *Who IS this beautiful man? Wait, what is going ON in Argentina? Hang on, who is this, please?*

I didn't know how to answer them.

*

Stephen Pyne wrote that humans can start fires at 'eccentric moments and with odd timings'. We can stop unwanted fires, control their size and heat level or send them billowing with the wind if we want.

'Not every spark cast ended in a flame or every fire in a flaming front, but ignition became as constant as human will desired.'

That night, Ale and I stayed across the road from Parque Salto Encantado. A local architect named Daniela Olivera had built an eco-friendly lodge with treehouse rooms on a patch of jungle passed down in her family. Ale pulled the truck into a huge grass clearing in front of the main lobby, a wooden house with a wide porch. I could hear the Cuña Pirú river somewhere in the tangle of vines beyond the grass.

'Here, we'll need these.' He handed me a walkie-talkie. 'There's no mobile service up here and wifi in the main lodge only.'

Daniela showed us to two neighbouring treehouses. I climbed up to the top of mine, marvelling at her genius – the bedroom was spacious, with a double bed, flushable toilet and even a bathtub, all in a treetop. I lay for a while on the bed listening to birds squawking nearby and tried to calm my racing thoughts. What was Ale thinking? Was I making up the chemistry or was he feeling it all, too?

When evening fell, we met in the main lodge for dinner home-cooked by Daniela. She was patient with my unprac-tised Spanish, listened carefully while I introduced myself and then explained that the lodge was not actually open for guests because she was tending to her ailing mother in the city. But Ale had called in a special favour for us to stay and she couldn't say no. I tried not to overthink the fact that he'd arranged for a treehouse lodge to be opened up specially for me.

We ate big bowls of tomato pasta and roasted aubergine while the evening darkened outside and the two of them rattled away in Spanish. Later, when we were alone at the table, Ale played songs for me on his phone.

'You should hear this one,' he said, 'Paula Fernandes. She is like the Shania Twain of Brazil.' The song started, a strong voice and soaring melody that I immediately loved. It was a live recording with the audience roaring beneath the vocals. As it played, Ale translated:

Quero acordar todo dia. 'I want to wake up every day . . .'

Pra te fazer todo o meu amor. 'To make you all of my love.'

The cold fever hit my neck again, the room suddenly hot and too bright. *It's all in your head. Don't get a crush on your colleague who lives a million miles away.*

Later, we turned all of the lights off and stood on the grass in the middle of the clearing. There was no Moon, only soft starlight. Ale set up his tripod and took photos of the Milky Way while I milled around trying to keep my cool and pretending everything was normal by taking pictures of the sky with my phone.

'You should put it on a tripod. The pictures will be much better,' he said.

'I'm not really a photographer. I don't have the patience to fiddle with settings. But I will stay here and stare at the sky while you do!' I laughed.

'Here, come and see.' He stood close to me and displayed one of the pictures he'd just taken of a deep-blue sky filled with zillions of stars.

'So . . .' He stared through the evening like he could see into my soul. 'How is the darkness here?'

Small details rushed into frame. His strong jaw, the curve of his nose outlined in starlight. I took a breath, sure he would kiss me.

'It's amazing . . .'

At that moment, Daniela emerged from the lodge carrying camp chairs and a flask.

'Ahora chicos. Un mate!' She couldn't see how close we were in the dark and brushed past me, holding out the cup of yerba mate in Ale's direction.

In the night, I lay awake in the dark on my bed high up in the treehouse listening to a chorus of crickets and frogs somewhere down by the riverside. Was Ale awake, too? Was he thinking about what almost happened? *I still have the walkie-talkie*, I thought. *Maybe he wanted me to use it.*

But fear and self-doubt swept in and, eventually, I fell into a deep sleep.

In the morning, we went back to Yvytu Porá. Domingo was home this time.

'Ale! Ale! Ale!' Three of Domingo's kids ran over and climbed on Ale, knocking him backwards off the tree trunk where we were sitting. After they talked a while, we walked into the jungle, the kids each holding Ale's hands. I followed behind snapping photos and trying to make mental notes, but feeling too distracted by how much the kids loved him.

Later, we drank cups of tereré, a Guaraní summer drink made of iced yerba mate and fruit juice, and ate hunks of boiled cassava dipped in honey that some of the men had foraged from the forest that morning. Domingo explained that many Guaraní communities in that area have a close relationship with bees, particularly the native *Melipona* honeybees, which are stingless and make their hives inside tree trunks. In addition to foraging honey, they use beeswax for medicines and rituals and make candles for nighttime ceremonies and blessings.

He then told a Guaraní story:

'At the beginning of time, several gods and spirits roamed the Earth, led by a good spirit and an evil spirit. When the people were going through great difficulties, a girl was born as the Goddess of Sleep. She taught the people to relate the stars in the sky with the climate, plants and animals of Earth. From that time, the sky became the basis of all Guaraní knowledge – activities like fishing, hunting and gathering followed the fluctuations of celestial cycles.

But the evil spirit fell in love with the Sleep Goddess and abducted her, so the gods punished him by giving him seven monstrous sons. Over time, the sons caused discord and fighting in the village. To restore order, a beautiful woman named Porãsy offered to sacrifice herself, adorning herself with flowers, feathers and perfume and luring the sons into a cave. The villagers lit a fire and sealed them all inside using boulders. At dawn, Porãsy's spirit rose from the cave into the heavens in the form of colourful smoke, transforming into the planet Venus, the Morning Star. The sons were consumed by fire for seven days and nights and eventually ascended to heaven, forming a star group called Eichu Jasy, or the Honeycomb. When this cluster appears for the first time before sunrise, it marks the beginning of our Guaraní new year.'

'The Honeycomb,' Ale added, 'is a star group you probably know by the name Pleiades – the Seven Sisters.'

'First Fire' appears in the fossil record around the same time plants began to grow on land some 470 million years ago. Plants released oxygen as a waste product into Earth's atmosphere and, when it accumulated above 13 per cent of the air, spontaneous wildfire became possible. Charcoal has been present in the fossil record ever since. Fire and life are inextricably bound together in Earth's story.

'It's too hot. We need the rains to come.' Ale took a long drag of his cigarette and stubbed it out into the red dirt with his toe, then poured a fresh mate. We pulled the truck up to a petrol station and, as it was filling, he washed the windscreen with a scrubber from beside the pump. I sat in the cab and tried not to stare. Why was everything he did so attractive?

A small disaster had struck. We couldn't go back to the treehouse that night as planned. Daniela's mother had taken a bad turn, and she had to rush home. Ale didn't have a contingency – we'd have to stay at his house in the city. He apologised over and over again, but I wasn't sorry; I was having the time of my life. He could have taken me to a cave and I would've followed happily along if there was mate and starlight and his sonorous Spanish.

We drove into Posadas, the provincial capital, as the sun was setting an orange that lit up the road like lava. Ale's house was on the outskirts of town, on a suburban street paved in red bricks the colour of the Misiones soil. Storm clouds had rolled in, making the dark darker and threatening but not delivering rain. His son, 11-year-old Ciro, and friends who'd been housesitting met us at the door along with screeches from Corcho, a little brown sausage dog who ran in and out with body-wiggling excitement. We sat in the backyard eating empanadas from a pizza box – Argentina's national snack, baked puff pastries filled with spiced minced beef. Ale told me I was seeing the real Argentina now and scolded me for not squeezing the lime into the empanada correctly.

Out in the darkness, over the city's edge, there was lightning again.

*

The final two days of the trip, we went south into neigh-bouring Corrientes province, to a wetland area called Iberá. Domingo came along, crammed into the back seat of the truck with Ciro and Ale's friend, Danny, who helped out as Ciro's nanny. As we drove out of Posadas, Ale turned the radio on and I took a selfie of us all, which he said was the 'photo of the trip' and texted to it his buddy who was the DJ on air. A few minutes later, we got a shout-out and song dedication.

Outside of Posadas, the terrain spread into a grassland, flat like rolled-out dough. After a few miles, lines of charred trees began to appear along the highway. Pine and euca-lyptus plantations, Ale explained, planted mostly for paper. Burnt trees filled both sides of the road, and charred grass, too. A managed fire had got out of control, he said, and blazed into the national park where we were headed.

'We had three months of blood-red moons that looked like eclipses from all the smoke in the atmosphere.'

Iberá Provincial Nature Reserve covers a vast corridor of Corrientes. It forms the largest protected natural park in Argentina and one of the biggest wetland areas in the world. An unpaved road led off from the highway, which turned into a sand track farther into the reserve that would've been impassable in a smaller car. Wading birds stood in pockets of water that glimmered in the grass. A family of daytime owls kept watch on a fence. And then, splayed across the road ahead, a caiman alligator – called yacaré in Guaraní, Domingo told me.

In the middle of the national park, a smaller, privately owned reserve contained the only accommodation. Managed by Alejandra Boloqui and her husband Cepi, the Reserva Don Luis and Wild Wetlands Lodge had several wood cabins on a plot of solid ground surrounded by swamps. A family of resident capybara were munching the lawn when we pulled in. They looked like guinea pigs the size of labradors and were completely unbothered when I approached to take a picture.

After nightfall, Cepi cooked a huge asado, the famous Argentinean meat grill, and we scarfed down lomo, chorizo and ribs at a long outdoor table, the aromas of meat smoke and oily charcoal covering our clothes. All the staff and a few people who were staying in the guest cabins joined us, and then Ale set up his camera and gave a stargazing tour, pointing out constellations that were only visible in the Southern Hemisphere. These were stars with unfamiliar names to me: Tucana, the toucan; Cruz, the southern cross; Carina, the ship. And in between them, the two fuzzy Magellanic Clouds, which looked like optical illusions or eyeglass smudges.

Ale called them by their Spanish name – las nubes or 'the clouds' – explaining they were galaxies between 150,000 and 200,000 light years away. I thought about what Uktam had told me up on Mount Maidanak in Uzbekistan. The light hitting our eyes tonight had left those galaxies 150,000 years ago. What was happening on Earth back then? Our most ancient ancestors, early Homo sapiens, were just migrating out of Africa into the Mediterranean. They were making rudimentary hand-axes and flint tools. The earliest Europeans already knew how to make fires. They were sharing knowledge and looking up at this same sky.

It had taken the light of the Magellanic Clouds all that time – most of human history – to travel from there to us, on a steamy night in Argentina. The photons entering my eyes were as old as humanity and unique, those particles of light finding me specifically.

Suddenly, I felt overwhelmed and needed to cry. I walked around the back of a van and stood in the shadows, away from the group, their laughter scattering over the wetlands out into the night. It was all such a gift – to see the stars, to stand in the presence of friends and strangers, share stories around the fire and cook meat together, to laugh and take photos and feel the tingle of an almost-kiss.

I kept staring upwards and let the tears fall. Then Ale came around calling my name. He wanted to know if I was okay, and I said I was but that sometimes I got a little overwhelmed by the sky and needed a deep breath. Could he come over, he wanted to know. Of course, I said, and he dragged his tripod into my dark patch and aimed it at the sky.

'You can cry if you need to,' he said. 'I understand.'

'There are just so many stars here,' my voice wavered. 'I feel a little dizzy.'

'Well,' he chuckled, 'I've been told I have that effect . . .'

*

'Something had to jolt and jostle the land for it to accept so startling a change,' wrote Pyne. 'That something, of course, was fire.'

The temperature reached 50°C on the final day and I couldn't move. My legs were covered in mosquito bites and the single dusty floor fan in my cabin was doing very little other than creating a hot wind. We'd all decided to ride out the depths of the afternoon with a siesta.

I couldn't sleep in the heat, and was just lying around, so I took a picture of my sweaty face and posted it to Instagram. Ale responded to it with a 'shocked' emoji, so I DM'd him back a picture of my mosquito-bitten legs. A few minutes later, he appeared at the screen door of the cabin holding a large cool box.

'I can't believe you are suffering like this and did not say anything. This is unacceptable. Here ...' he opened the box to reveal bottles of ice water, juice and cold fruit, and then set to spraying my legs with his homemade bug repellent.

'Now rest and keep drinking. And if you need anything, please call me right away. I will be in the main house with Alejandra. We are talking and drinking tereré, and you can join if you feel like it.'

After he left, I tried to remember a time when a man had rushed to take care of me or spoil me like that and couldn't think of one.

I texted him: *Thank you for that. You being so chivalrous is making my crush on you worse. Laugh emoji, cry emoji, sparkle emoji.*

A few seconds later, he replied: *I don't know how to be any other way. Don't worry. You are in complete trust here. I'm, I think, a gentleman.*

Much later, I ventured down to the main house where everyone was sitting on the back porch overlooking the swamp, with birds swirling into the dusky sky looking for insects. Ale made a show of my bug bites and insisted on spraying me fully again with repellent. I really didn't know what kind of strange flirting this was, but I liked it.

That night, Ale and Domingo were to give a full Cielo Guaraní event for all of the lodge's guests and staff. There were two large families with kids of various ages, plus volunteer staff members who lived onsite for several months of the year doing maintenance and nature conservation work.

Nothing had happened beyond our flirting, and, by that time, I was sure it wouldn't. It was the final evening and, with so many people around, I knew there would be no chance for a private moment.

After dinner, I stood at a fence near the edge of the property and watched the darkness stretch out across the wetland to the horizon. Nearby, Domingo had lit a small torch and was muttering prayers and wafting the smoke along the property line: a smudge. He was asking the fire gods for protection and permission to conduct a gathering at night.

Ale came and stood beside me and asked how I was. I

knew he was getting at a deeper question. But how could I reply?

I am feeling all the things. I wish I didn't have to go. Why haven't we said what we wanted to say? Why didn't you kiss me yet? Will you now?

But none of those words came. Domingo moved closer and then, without hesitation, began encircling us with a fragrant smoke whose scent was rich and unfamiliar. Eucalyptus maybe, or palo santo?

Domingo approached, and in a whisper, Ale translated that he would give me a blessing, then Domingo placed a palm on my forehead and wafted the smoke all around me, speaking words in Guaraní, moving his palm from my head to my heart and back. He then spoke those few words to Ale in Spanish about my feverish body and some for Ale himself that I did not understand.

I stood there for a while afterwards trying to calm my body and catch my breath.

Camp chairs had been set up on a strip of sand that jutted out into the swamp water. The lights on the whole property were switched off and the families took their seats while Ale introduced the night sky, pointing out stars and constellations with a green laser pointer and also explaining the problem of light pollution, how even here on this remote strip of land in the country's largest national park, we could see the tiniest bit of skyglow from a city a hundred kilometres away. Then Domingo introduced himself in his soft, accented Spanish, explaining the Guaraní stories of the night sky.

'These two white clouds – which Alejandro called the "Magellanic Clouds" – for we Guaraní, these are torches left by our ancestors. The ancestors also did not call it the Milky Way, they called it Mborevi Rape – or the road of the tapir god. When the ancestors leave this life, they follow that road to return to the sky, where we are all from. The two clouds we call torches – these have been left by our ancestors to show us the way home when we pass over.'

By the time Domingo finished his presentation, I had been swarmed by thousands of mosquitos and bitten through my clothes. The lights stayed off and Ale set up his telescope, the kids taking turns for a look. I was ill at ease and had a pulsing energy welling up that I couldn't identify. I felt antsy and needed to get away from all the people, so I walked towards the end of the sand spit, as far as I could go, and looked north. Stars fell to the horizon, which was flat in every direction. Clouds had begun to gather and then, there again, a flash. Lightning. It was very far away. Probably many miles, but out here the light travelled far. Another flash.

Then, the world closed around me fast. Stars faded away. In my ears, a rushing noise. I felt pulled forwards as if speeding through a tunnel, or like my body was trying to come out of its skin. Nothing was real, there was no time, no gravity, no sound except the roaring freight train in my ears and some disembodied voice in my head saying this was okay. I could go, I could be pulled onwards, outwards, to somewhere else. This was all there was. Nothing and everything, everywhere, all at once. I wanted to go wherever it was, to the nothing, to the pulling.

It felt wonderful. I leaned forward into the void.

'Megan. Megan? Hey, where are you? Are you here?'

Ale's voice cut through the roar. I could still feel it pulling, I could still go with it if I wanted to. Or I could come back. I knew I needed to come back, but the pulling felt like the most ecstatic home, and I wanted to stay out there.

You have to go back, I heard in my mind.

'I'm here,' I croaked out loud. 'I'm out here, Ale.'

'Where are you?'

'I'm not sure. I wasn't here for a minute, but I am here.'

'Where did you go?' he sounded worried. I had to go back.

'I don't know.'

'A bad place or a good place?' he asked.

'I don't know,' I said again, pulling myself around towards the sound of his voice. 'Good place. I think it was good.'

Ale drove the white truck into the tiny departures area at Posadas airport and lifted my suitcase from the back seat. He looked into my eyes, saying everything without any words. Holding his gaze was like looking into the universe; beautiful and heavy. I couldn't carry it all and had to look away.

We had left everything unsaid and unexplored. After meeting the void the night before, I'd found my way back to my bed and lay in the dark shivering in the heat, not sure where I was or what time it was. I did not sleep and did not feel tired. Whatever mental break or cosmic experience I'd been so anxious about having in the dark room, I'd instead had at the edge of an Argentinean swamp.

Ale had pulled me back from the something, or somewhere, and I'd never fully be able to explain or understand it. Much later, he would tell me that Domingo and many of the Guaraní consider Iberá to be a portal to another realm and that lightning was the gods passing through it.

We hugged and I shuffled my suitcase around nervously.

'You will come back again. When it's not so hot next time.' He smiled and looked sad.

'I will definitely come back.' I hugged him again.

'We should take a picture,' he said, holding the camera up for a selfie. And after that, I grabbed my things and ran into the airport fighting tears, trying not to think about what might've been.

My plane took off through dark clouds and skated over a big thunderhead pouring sheets of rain somewhere south of Posadas.

By the time I reached Buenos Aires, Ale had blown up my phone with text messages. The rains had arrived in Posadas. *You came to research fire and it held off all that time and then poured as soon as you left*, he wrote with a video of water cascading off the roof of his house into the backyard where we'd eaten empanadas.

The flood of texts continued for twenty-four hours, then weeks, as we confessed our feelings, regrets about what didn't happen, flirtations and promises to visit each other soon.

I spent one night in Buenos Aires, nosing through antique bookshops and going to a show at one of the tango clubs I'd dreamed about, and then took a ferry across the Río de la Plata to Colonia del Sacramento in Uruguay to meet Fefo Bouvier. Another dark sky advocate, Fefo was a well-known astrophotographer whose photographs of the Uruguayan sky had been featured by NASA.

At sunset, Fefo and I went for dinner at a restaurant overlooking the estuary. The sky was the colour of ripe peaches and the stars were coming out. We chose a table near the edge of the patio with a wide view and talked about Fefo's adventures into the Uruguayan wilderness to take photos.

A text came through from Ale – he was going out to try to catch a glimpse of the International Space Station, which would be passing overhead in about an hour. I said Fefo and I were going to try to see it, too, and Ale replied with a single sentence:

We are far apart, but we are under the same sky.

10

HOPE

Chicago

Quiana couldn't sleep. A light was flickering outside her bedroom window. The light was from a primary school across the street from her house, empty of children at 3 a.m. The light seeped through her thin blinds and cast flashes on the wall. She closed her eyes but, no matter how tight, flashing still danced through her brain. The hours crept closer to her 7 a.m. alarm; she had an important high school science test the next day. This was nothing new; the light had been flashing for months, and Quiana had got used to these sleepless nights. But arriving at school groggy was starting to take its toll.

A few miles away, another student named Ashley lived in an apartment building next to a huge airport. Light from the runways poured into her windows at all hours. Like most in their underserved Chicago neighbourhood,

Ashley's family made do with what they had. Curtains couldn't contain the light spill, so they taped black garbage bags over all their windows. This also kept out sunlight during the day, but Ashley's family worked long hours and she was busy at school maintaining good grades. The garbage bags weren't pretty and they made her mom feel ashamed, but at least they could sleep.

Both girls were students at Lawndale High School in Little Village, a predominantly Mexican-American neighbourhood in southwest Chicago. They would eventually become friends and anti-light-pollution activists through the Youth Organization for Lights Out, an after-school programme run by the Adler Planetarium. And that's where they became part of my story.

A few years ago, I took an astrophysics course at the Royal Observatory in London. The observatory opened in 1676 on a hill in Greenwich Park beside the River Thames and was the working home of Britain's Astronomers Royal. Today, it overlooks the towers of Canary Wharf, where bank and insurance offices stay lit all night, but for centuries, Greenwich was a royal palace surrounded by hilly countryside. It became an important shipyard and home of the Royal Naval College, with the observatory contributing timekeeping and celestial navigation that enabled the British to colonise the world by sea. With the advent of longitude, the Prime Meridian was placed here because most of the world's maps and navigation charts already used Greenwich as the starting point, and the world's foundational time zone eventually took its name – Greenwich Mean Time. You might say Greenwich was the Western world's original stargazing zone.

My astronomy course was held on weeknights in February, which gave us access to the park after dark when it was normally closed. The promenade along the Prime Meridian, which during the day filled up with tourists photographing themselves in two hemispheres at once, was still and sleepy. The lights of Canary Wharf glinted in the sharp winter air. There were no stars to be found amid the skyglow – instead, we looked at pictures of stars on a projector in a classroom.

The working observatory at Greenwich closed in 1998 and was turned into a museum. Light pollution was a growing problem, and the stars had already disappeared from London. Professional observations of the night sky were moved to remote observatories away from light.

The idea of doing real astronomy in a big city now is absurd. But London isn't the only metropolis that was once brimming with astronomers – in the nineteenth century, there were observatories in all the biggest cities in Europe and the United States, including one at Adler Planetarium in Chicago. Most of them aren't working much today, if at all, but Adler is still an active science institution with a planetarium, observatory and anti-light-pollution programmes, including the Youth Organization for Lights Out, or YOLO, the programme led by local high school students. I also happened to have a dark sky friend who worked there.

Ken Walczak and I had been emailing for several years about the deeper philosophical reasons for rampant light pollution. I could thread several of those conversations back to the idea for this book. The year I began writing, two of the YOLO students won a DarkSky International award for their efforts to raise awareness about light pollution in Chicago. The next generation, undaunted by the screwed-up, overlit world they'd inherited, were doing what they could to shift things in their own community. The award winners were the two girls, Quiana and Ashley.

In 1913, a German engineer named Oskar von Miller had an idea: he wanted to create a modern version of an orrery, a solar system model that worked on gears. Such models had been in existence at least since the Greeks created the Antikythera mechanism, a hand-powered gear system that could predict astronomical positions and eclipses in the second century BCE. By von Miller's time, in the early 1900s, there was a variety of large-scale orreries in Europe and beyond, including one in the Dutch city of Franeker built by Eise Eisinga in 1781. Eisinga's was so big it took over his entire living room with a complex gear system on which the model still rotates today. Von Miller's vision was different. He worked with an engineer on a method to project an image of the night sky onto an indoor dome. They called it a planetarium – the first one projected 4,900 stars and the second one 8,956 stars. The concept became popular across Europe, and by 1929, there were fifteen planetaria in Germany, two in Italy, one in Russia and one in Austria.

Enter Max Adler, an American executive from Chicago who heard about these new planetaria from a friend who'd visited one in Munich. Adler was enthralled with the idea of projecting the stars onto a dome and immediately wanted to bring one to Chicago, which was at that time developing several science museums. This was at a period in history when electricity was spreading rapidly and outdoor light at night was a growing novelty. The first neon sign had been installed in New York's Times Square in 1924, advertising the automaker Willys–Overland, and by the 1940s, all the big cities, including Chicago, were ablaze with bulbs and neon lights. A planetarium offered a chance for urban dwellers to learn about the stars right there in the newly glittering city.

Adler went to Germany to see the planetarium first hand, along with his cousin, an architect named Ernest Grunsfeld Jr, whom he later commissioned to create the design. Adler outfitted his Chicago planetarium with astronomical in-struments purchased from Amsterdam. When it opened on 12 May 1930 – Max Adler's sixty-fourth birthday – Adler Planetarium became the first of its kind in the Western Hemisphere.

The planetarium was built on Northerly Island, a human-made recreational island created by the city of Chicago for the 1925 World's Fair. It juts in an L formation into Lake

Michigan, just south of downtown. Along with the Field Museum and Shedd Aquarium, it created Chicago's new museum trifecta.

My return home to London had been jarring after so many dark places. The stars didn't sparkle overhead. Orion's belt and the Pleiades were faint. The Milky Way was completely gone. I went for a night walk in my local park on Blythe Hill and strained to see the cosmos. Instead, it was just insipid yellow-grey skyglow and London's tallest skyscraper, the Shard, flaring with a new light installation.

Ale and I continued to call each other; the three-hour time difference between Posadas and London didn't seem so big, but the ocean between us did. I had been on my own for such a long time that this new shared reality was upending. I made plans to go back to Argentina, not sure how or if we would make it work. All I knew was how I'd felt, calm and sure next to him in the dark, and how he'd pulled me back when I'd faced the void. It was a sudden new path and another I would have to walk in the dark.

Just as the hopeless, grey London skies were starting to cast a shadow over my mood, an email from Ken dropped into my inbox. The YOLO students were starting a new programme, he said, and might be getting a NASA grant to work on an environmental justice light pollution project for their neighbourhood. They were also building sky cameras to measure the light dome of Chicago. Did I want to come and hang out at the high school and meet the community?

Obviously.

I booked my flights that afternoon.

In Chicago, when someone says 'la veintiséis', they're referring to the neighbourhood of Little Village and its main street, West 26th Street – an arrow-straight main drag lined with taquerias, Mexican bakeries and quinceañera dress shops. The area was populated by Czech and Polish immigrants in the 1800s, but, by the 1960s, those families had moved elsewhere, and many Mexican families began moving in. Resources for the neighbourhood were limited, as politicians gave preference to wealthier, white-majority districts.

Until the 1990s, all of Little Village was served by a single, overcrowded high school. The neighbourhood parents came together to petition then-mayor Richard Daley to build the new school he'd promised during his election campaign. But several years passed and there was still no school, so in 2001, a group of community members staged a hunger strike. They set up camp on a vacant strip of land next to an old cooking-oil plant and painted signs that said 'SOLIDARIDAD ES UNA ARMA' / 'SOLIDARITY IS A WEAPON' and 'Daley we hold YOU ACCOUNTABLE'. Through days of rain and cold weather, they ate nothing – mothers, grandparents, neighbours and high school students. The strike proved enough to prod the mayor and Chicago Public Schools to fulfil their promise, and in 2005, the Lawndale High School campus opened, housing four new secondary schools focused on multicultural arts, world languages, social justice and STEM. The community had ensured a future for the next generation.

I was met at the airport by Ken's colleague, Waleska Do Valle Santos, who manages the YOLO programme, a co-ordinated effort among students from several high schools in the area. As we drove to Little Village, she told me about her life growing up in São Paulo, Brazil, which she said gave her a deep understanding of the Little Village students' urban lives, and credence as a Latina woman working in a predominantly Mexican neighbourhood.

It had been decades since I was inside an American high school, and Lawndale was nothing like the tiny religious school I'd been sent to in an evangelical church. Shiny, modern buildings sprawled across several acres along with well-kept football and baseball fields. I followed Waleska into the main entrance and there my stomach dropped: confronting us was an airport-style metal detector staffed by a uniformed security guard.

Of course, I knew there were metal detectors in schools now, but I'd never encountered one. I'd graduated in 1998, the year before two teenage boys took an arsenal of pistols and shotguns into a high school in Colorado, murdering thirteen people and injuring twenty-one. The Columbine massacre became the deadliest school shooting in US history and set off a wave of copycat events that haven't abated.

Metal detectors and security stations have become a fact of life in US schools.

It was 3.15 p.m. and everything was quiet, but soon a bell sounded and teenagers came pouring out of every door, filling the halls with baggy jeans, low-slung backpacks and chatter that reminded me, also, that some things about high school do not change.

'Let's gather around in a circle,' Waleska said, indicating for the students to pull their desks together. We were in a literature classroom after hours, the walls covered in classic film posters and book covers. I squeezed my forty-something body into a desk with 'AT + JL' carved into the wood. We went around introducing ourselves, the students describing their experiences with light pollution and the YOLO programme, which had included field trips to dark sky areas outside of Chicago to see the stars. Growing up in this deeply urban part of the city, the trips had been most of the students' first chances to see the Milky Way. One girl laughed, remembering that her mother couldn't believe they found a place without street lights. A young freshman said she was excited to be in the programme because it gave her a chance to learn why the stars have disappeared in Chicago and to go see them in a dark place. Another boy commented that he joined the programme because 'we ruined our planet to a point where we can't see stars' and he wanted to do something about that.

They talked excitedly about a trip they'd taken a few

weeks earlier to Middle Fork River Forest Preserve, a certified Dark Sky Park about 120 miles southwest of Chicago.

'It was my first time seeing stars in the sky and it felt unreal,' said one boy dreamily. 'It felt like a little globe. It was amazing seeing that many stars.'

They regaled me with their feelings of awe and peace on seeing the Milky Way for the first time, their experiences of surprise, uncertainty and even fear at just how dark it really was and, importantly, a sense of togetherness as they lay on their backs and saw their first shooting stars.

Ashley and Quiana, who had been part of the programme for several years and had slotted naturally into leadership roles, sat next to each other and explained the programme's goals for the upcoming year, which were to begin working with other schools in Little Village, especially younger, primary-school-aged students.

'In order for us to help improve other schools, we must make sure that ours is not polluting,' Quiana said, explaining how they had completed a lighting inventory of Lawndale's grounds. They obtained blueprints of the school and drew their own maps, cataloguing each light and fixture and noting its characteristics, whether it was glaring into the sky or shielded down, whether it was a bright white light or an amber one, and if it had problems like flickering. The next steps, she said, would be to work with their school administrators and the public school system to adapt the lights at Lawndale to dark sky-friendly ones. Armed with the know-how and experience, they were taking this model to other schools in the area, and were designing flyers about light pollution and its impacts to distribute on their own campus and at four other schools in Little Village.

The sun was already dropping into a soft sunset as we left the school, now silent and drowsy for the night. Outside lights were starting to switch on. Quiana and Ashley pointed out a few that they'd marked in their inventory, then said hasty goodbyes and jumped in their parents' cars. As she drove me to my hotel, Waleska said they'd had word that they'd received the NASA grant and would be using the funding to implement a three-year environmental justice initiative within YOLO. The result would be a dashboard visualising how artificial light at night corresponds to social demographics, health and crime data across Chicago. This would be a crucial tool for educators, public administrators and the government to understand Chicago's light pollution problem and its impacts on specific communities. Ashley, Quiana and the other YOLO students would help build the dashboard along with a new light pollution curriculum for Chicago's schools.

The next day, I went to Adler with Ken. Standing on a strip of island east of the city, the planetarium has the perfect vantage of the Chicago skyline. The dome of the observatory was closed – and anyway, I couldn't imagine how the telescopes would be able to do much science once the Magnificent Mile was all lit up with its nightly parade of cars, rattling L trains and showgoers pouring into neon-lit theatres and pizzerias.

I spent the morning with one of Adler's other teen out-reach programmes, Far Horizons, a cohort of high school science students from across the city. I was introduced to the group by Lauren Wisbrock, a former high school biology teacher who now leads the programme. The students showed me how they were using special cameras they built at Adler, called Ground Observation Network (GONet) cameras, which take 360-degree images of the night sky. They explained how they use the GONet cameras to measure and understand light pollution across Chicago and shared pictures they had taken of the lighting and night sky in their neighbourhoods. They were using the GONets to conduct a study of the ecological impacts of light pollution on urban tree life cycles. Lauren said they were currently learning to accurately use the cameras, and next, they would collect the data and practise communicating their findings about light pollution to the public. It made me feel hopeful to see the next generation hands-on in learning not only scientific protocols but also how to communicate and reach public ears.

That afternoon, I wandered through the planetarium's museum exhibition, which told the story of the YOLO students from Little Village who were helping to combat light pollution in their school.

There on the walls were Ashley and Quiana, their stories in their own words, printed in English and Spanish alongside photos they'd taken around Little Village. Glowing street lights, a petrol station ablaze with LEDs, schools and empty sports fields shining for no one. I was struck by one of Ashley, her back to the camera, standing on an empty railway track facing downtown Chicago, towards a fence of impenetrably bright skyscrapers that cast a pink glow into low-slung clouds. She looked unafraid and steady, with the will of her parents' generation – the courage of the Little Village elders who were willing to starve themselves to ensure their children's future. Now, those children had a NASA grant and were mapping Chicago's demographics and its light pollution to create a tool that would help make a difference in people's lives.

After Chicago, I went to New Mexico to stay at my sister's house on the land where we grew up. My best friend Lauren drove in from Kansas and we all sat out on the back patio soaking in the hot tub, looking up at the Milky Way, talking about adventures, heartbreaks, the sky, the faraway cars whose lights cast eerie shadows on the house, and the UFOs I'd seen with my stepdad there so many years ago. It felt like a everything had come full circle.

I went on from there to Tucson to meet my colleagues at DarkSky International headquarters: Ruskin, Bettymaya, Drew, Natasha, Michael, Amber, Abby. They'd called in favours with friends Spencer and Brian, who are rangers at Saguaro National Park just outside of town, recently certified as a Dark Sky Place. There would be a big potluck picnic. I drove the winding road over Gates Pass, a rocky, dry mountain filled in every direction with towering

saguaro cacti, their branches stretching up like trium-
phant arms.

We met up at a picnic area in the far reaches of the park
and chose a table that looked across a vast expanse of desert,
spreading out containers of homemade guacamole, maca-
roni and cheese, fruit and sweets. The dry, cool air was quiet
as we ate and watched the sun go down.

So what does it all mean, they wanted to know. *What have
you learned from all this nightfaring?* I told them about Ulugh
Beg, the old Uzbek observatory, the starry Japanese beach
full of hooting owls. About Ale and the lightning and the
Argentinean fire blessing. The monk on the Himalayan
mountaintop. How I'd listened for nightbirds and met
Māori stargazers, seen all the versions of the Pleiades and
learned all their names. Felt both the prickly fear and the
warm comfort of the dark.

I'd stood in the night with strangers and friends. Learned
their stories, our collective myths and the old ways. I'd
seen strange apparitions and eavesdropped on wolves in a
primordial dawn howl. Felt my heart beating, my aliveness
under a blanket of sky. Lain on my own, sightless in a small
room, and let the dark nothingness of existence settle over
me. When I looked around the table at my friends, drawn
here together by a love of the night sky, I was certain how
darkness connects us all – the stars, the storytelling and the
great unknown.

Becoming comfortable in the dark requires trust, I told them.
You put one foot in front of the other, the path revealing

itself as you walk. There is no way to control the outcome and no way to light the path ahead of time. You rest in not knowing – how a life will unfold, what terrain your feet will next land on, where predators might stalk you, if your health may fail, or when love could find you and if it will stand the test of time. With all our light-switching, we cannot – will not – ever predict the future. We are just here, walking together in the dark.

I was reminded of that warm New Zealand summer evening on my first trip, when I learned about whānau, the Māori term for your community or chosen family. It felt like I'd built a whole new whānau in the dark – the joyous welcome and gracious embrace of advocates and night-lovers around the world who joined me in looking up at the sky. Even with such different backgrounds, ways of speaking and home landscapes, we all looked at the same sky and accepted the mystery of existence.

In the end, my journey through the night was one of connection. To myself and others. To our stories, our histories, our collective birth from the depths of a shadowy womb. Are we even alive if we cannot stop and experience it fully? The darkness holds it all. The potential, the discoveries, the legends and the purpose of life rest in the shadow beyond what we can see.

As the daylight dimmed, we climbed to the top of a small outcropping. Bettymaya, who is for my money the world's best night-sky photographer, snapped lavender-hued photos of us each backlit by twinkling stars. The night fell, alive with our laughter ringing across the desert. *This darkness*, I told them, *feels friendly and warm*.

Ranger Brian pointed to rocks where spiral-shaped petroglyphs had been carved. He said they were around 1,500 years old and likely related to the solstices. The spirals looked just like the ones I'd seen on the Boheh Stone in Ireland. But these were drawn by Ancestral Puebloan people – the ancient ancestors of the Native Americans who, before my own family was born, lived on the land where I would play in the dirt, hear the hiss of a rattlesnake's tail and see the stars through my dad's telescope. Two ancient civilisations – Celtic and Puebloan – continents and generations apart from each other and also from my friends and me. All of us connected across time and space by the star-splashed night.

ACKNOWLEDGEMENTS

Thank you first to my agent, Jack Fogg, who believed in my writing even before this book was a proposal – none of this would have happened without you. I'm also grateful to Zoë Pagnamenta at Calligraph for representing the book in the US. Thanks to Assallah Tahir at Simon & Schuster UK and Gwen Hawkes at Hachette US for commissioning it, and to Kate Harvey for her incredible edits and un-wavering support. Thanks to Maudisa King, Kerri Sharp and the Simon & Schuster UK team, and to Morgan Spehar, Maddie Caldwell and the Grand Central team in the US for helping bring this book to fruition.

Thank you to the Society of Authors and the Authors' Foundation for awarding me a 2024 Authors' Foundation Grant, which helped fund this research. Thanks also to the British Library, Lewisham Libraries, Goldsmiths College and the Weston Library Special Collections at the Bodleian Library, Oxford.

I owe a huge debt of gratitude to the many people and organisations who hosted, guided and welcomed me into their communities, projects and lives. Adrien Vilquin Barrajon and the folks from Dark Sky Project; Sonal, Paras, Simar, Nikki and Dorjay at Astrostays, who were heroes when I got sick in Ladakh; Sophie Ibbotson for her endless support; Viktoriya Yalanskaya and all the folks at Ulugh Beg Astronomical Institute; Ken Walczak, Waleska Do Valle Santos, Lauren Wisbrock and everyone at Adler; Kloster Gut Saunstorf; Hoshinoya Resorts; Jane Collyer and Gemma Minto at Travel PR; Katie Silcox at *Citizen Femme* for the Japan commission; Georgia MacMillan and Ged Dowling in Ireland; Valerio Reale at Rewilding Apennines; and the folks at Wildlife Adventures for the wolfish days in Italy.

I owe a lot to Fabio, Melanie, Anaïk, Sudha, Karen and the team at Unearthodox for their inspiration and support in working with me so flexibly while I wrote.

My life would not be the same if it weren't for my family at DarkSky International – Bettymaya, Ruskin, Drew, Michael, Amber, Natasha, Abby and Chris: I admire all of you deeply. Also, Brian and Spencer from Saguaro National Park – thank you for the epic dark sky picnic. Robert Massey and Marieta Valdivia Lefort at the Royal Astronomical Society, as well as John Barentine, Dan Oakley and all the DarkSky UK peeps for teaching me so much about policy and astronomy. And the hundreds of dark sky advocates around the world, including Fefo in Uruguay, Samyukta and Carol in Kenya, Kerem Asfuroglu, Dani Robertson, Marcelo Souza, and Paulina and Pearl.

ACKNOWLEDGEMENTS

Paul Bogard is the OG writer on this topic, and his book, *The End of Night*, was a huge inspiration to me.

I must say cheers to Annie and the baristas at Fred's in Crofton Park for keeping me supplied with flat whites and encouragement on many hard writing days.

To my girls, my soul family: Lauren, Summer, Kristen, Stephanie, Caroline, Kimbers, Pip, GG, Emma, and Mercedes (who also got me to Tanzania) – you all keep me alive. Peter G, Macron, and Revillator – thank you for being great AF drinking buddies; and Oli Smith, thank you for being my writing crush and for commiserating about the book process. And to Stephen Lioy, for that night under the stars in Kyrgyzstan, which got me thinking about all of this years ago.

Tom, I'm forever grateful we exist in the world at the same time, and, even still, you provide the soundtrack to everything.

Ale, thank you for jumping into the void with me.

Most of all, my deepest gratitude goes to my family: Jane and Dave, for always having my room ready; Dad and Kathryn, for your support and for living in the most beautiful place on Earth; Juels, Dave and Prudence, for creating a safe space under the New Mexico stars; and Dan, who would be proud that I did, in the end, just travel and write.

Some of the author's advance from this book has been donated to Cielo Guaraní for the preservation of Indigenous sky knowledge in Argentina.

References

Online sources were accessed in December 2024.

Into the Dark

Cinzano, P. and Falchi, F. et al., 'The first World Atlas of the artificial night sky brightness', *Monthly Notices of the Royal Astronomical Society*, 328:3 (2001).

Falchi, Fabio et. al., 'The new world atlas of artificial night sky brightness', *Science Advances*, 2:6 (2016).

Falchi, Fabio and Salvador, Bará, 'Light pollution is skyrocketing', *Science*, 379:6629 (2023).

Heschong, Lisa, 'Day and Night, Life and Light', DarkSky International Under One Sky Global Conference, 15 Nov 2022, YouTube, https://www.youtube.com/watch?v=HWIAUiCDcGc/

Hopkins, Gerard Manley, 'The Starlit Night', *Poems and Prose*, (Penguin Classics, 1985).

Solnit, Rebecca, 'Hugging the Shadows – and basking in the dark', *Orion*, Jan/Feb 2005, p.13.

Swift, Taylor, 'Jack and I found ourselves back in New York, alone, recording every night, staying up late and exploring old memories and midnights past', Instagram, 21 Oct 2022, https://www.instagram.com/p/Cj9ir4EOrL4/?img_index=1/

Wordsworth, William, 'The Stars Are Mansions Built By Nature's Hand', https://allpoetry.com/The-Stars-Are-Mansions-Built-By-Nature's-Hand/

1. HOME

Anthony, Andrew, 'Urban foxes: are they "fantastic" or a growing menace?' *Guardian*, 15 Oct 2022.

Baker, Hazel, London History Podcast. 'Episode 96. Gas Lamps of Westminster', https://londonguidedwalks.co.uk/podcast/episode-96-gas-lamps-of-westminster/

BBC, 'The repair team preserving an 18th Century home', 26 Jul 2021, https://www.bbc.co.uk/news/in-pictures-57824929/

Beaumont, Matthew, *Night Walking: A Nocturnal History of London* (London, Verso, 2016).

Bogard, Paul, *The End of Night: Searching for Natural Darkness in an Age of Artificial Light* (London, Fourth Estate, 2014).

Brightwell cum Sotwell Neighbourhood Plan, 2016–32, https://www.southoxon.gov.uk/wp-content/uploads/sites/2/2019/01/BCS-Neighbourhood-Plan-Referendum-Version-Report-amended-1-August-17.pdf/

Dill, Marie, National Association of Local Councils, private email: 'Press enquiry about street lighting in parishes/towns across Britain', 2021.

Earth Trust, 'Wittenham Clumps', https://earthtrust.org.uk/visit/wittenham-clumps/

Edwards, Nina, *Darkness: A Cultural History* (London, Reaktion Books Ltd, 2018).

Ekirch, A. Roger, *At Day's Close: A History of Nighttime* (London, Phoenix, 2006).

Jones, Richard, London Walking Tours, 'The Carting Lane Sewer Powered Gas Lamp', https://www.london-walking-tours.co.uk/secret-london/carting-lane-sewer-gas-lamp.htm/

Look Up London, 'Snuffers and Link-boys', 13 Dec 2016, https://lookup.london/snuffers-link-boys/

National Gas Museum, 'Gas Lighting: Resources for teachers', https://www.nationalgas.com/sites/default/files/documents/Gas%20Lighting_linked_v3.pdf/

Police, Fire and Crime Commissioner for Essex, 'Report finds no evidence that part-night lighting has an impact on crime levels',

6 Mar 2018, https://www.essex.pfcc.police.uk/news/report-finds-no-evidence-part-night-lighting-impact-crime-levels/

Schivelbusch, Wolfgang, *Disenchanted Night: The Industrialization of Light In the Nineteenth Century* (Berkeley and Los Angeles, California, University of California Press, 1995).

Stamp, Gavin, 'Dennis Severs obituary', *Guardian*, 10 Jan 2000.

Transport for London, 'LED street lighting trial assessment report', Mar 2011, https://content.tfl.gov.uk/LED-street-lighting-trial-report.pdf

2. FAMILY

Campion, Nicholas, *Astrology and Cosmology in the World's Religions* (New York, New York University Press, 2012).

Dark Sky Project, 'Cātai Aroraki (Māori Astronomy)', https://www.darkskyproject.co.nz/our-story/

Dunlop, Ryan, 'Oamaru claims official steampunk world record from Guinness', *Stuff*, 15 Aug 2016, https://www.stuff.co.nz/timaru-herald/news/83162685/oamaru-claims-official-steampunk-world-record-from-guinness/

Dunn, Nick and Edensor, Tim, *Rethinking Darkness: Cultures, Histories, Practices* (Oxon, Abington, Routledge, 2021).

Egenes, John, *Man and Horse: The Long Ride Across America* (Delta Vee, 2017).

Eaves, Megan, 'Who Owns the Night Sky?', *Nightscape* (#106, Dec 2021).

Exploratorium, 'About Chaco Canyon: Ancient Chaco', https://annex.exploratorium.edu/chaco/HTML/canyon.html/

Federal Aviation Administration, 'Satellite Navigation – GPS – How It Works', https://www.faa.gov/about/office_org/headquarters_offices/ato/service_units/techops/navservices/gnss/gps/howitworks/

Field, John and Wassilieff, Maggy, 'Night sky – Seasonal stars: Interpretations of Orion', Te Ara – the Encyclopedia of New Zealand, http://www.TeAra.govt.nz/en/diagram/7917/interpretations-of-orion/

Hamacher, Duane with Elders and Knowledge Holders, *The First Astronomers: How Indigenous Elders read the stars* (Sydney, Allen & Unwin, 2022).

Harris, Pauline, Mātāmua, Rangi, et al., 'A review of Māori astronomy in Aotearoa–New Zealand', *Journal of Astronomical History and Heritage*, 16:3 (2013).

Leather, Kay and Hall, Richard, *Tātai Arorangi, Māori Astronomy: Work of the Gods* (New Zealand, Viking Sevenseas NZ, 2004).

Lee, Annette, 'Wicaŋhpi Oyate (Star People)', DarkSky International, Under One Sky Global Conference, 18 Nov 2020, YouTube, https://www.youtube.com/watch?v=u3cjiGOEQlw/

Magdalena, Federico V., 'Who is Enrique de Malacca in PH history?', *SunStar*, 8 Apr 2023, https://www.sunstar.com.ph/cebu/lifestyle/who-is-enrique-de-malacca-in-ph-history

Maryboy, Nancy C., Begay, David C., and Teren, Ashley C., *Seeing the Skies Through Navajo Eyes: An Introduction to Cross-Cultural Astronomy* (Friday Harbor, Washington, Indigenous Education Institute, 2017).

Massey University, 'Meet the man behind Matariki celebrations: Professor Rangi Mātāmua', 21 Jun 2022, https://www.massey.ac.nz/about/news/meet-the-man-behind-matariki-celebrations-professor-rangi-mātāmua/

Mātāmua, Rangi, *Matariki: The Star of the Year* (Wellington, Huia, 2017).

Moorfield, John C., 'Te Aka Māori Dictionary', 2003–23, https://maoridictionary.co.nz/

NASA and the Navajo Nation Project, 'Sq' Baa Hane', Story of the Stars', 2006, https://astrobiology.nasa.gov/education/nasa-and-the-navajo-nation/story-of-the-stars/

Norris, Ray, 'Australia's first astronomers', BBC Earth, https://www.bbcearth.com/news/australias-first-astronomers

Orbiting Now, Active Satellite Orbit Data, https://orbit.ingnow.com/

Rāwiri Taonui, 'Canoe navigation – Ocean voyaging', Te Ara – the

Encyclopedia of New Zealand, https://teara.govt.nz/en/ diagram/2222/maori-star-compass

Redford, Carol, 'Emu in the Sky | June', Astrotourism WA. 2018–2023, https://astrotourismwa.com.au/emu-in-the-sky/

Tohunga, 'The Wisdom of the Maori – The Call of the Stars', *The New Zealand Railways Magazine* 11:5 (1936).

Venkatesan, Aparna, 'The Cultural Relevance of Dark and Quiet Sky Protection' seminar, 31 May 2023, YouTube, https://www. youtube.com/watch?v=7TlmznywUYU/

Williamson, Ray A. and Farrier, Claire R., *Earth & Sky: Visions of the Cosmos in Native American Folklore* (Albuquerque, New Mexico, University of New Mexico Press, 1992).

Whitfield, Peter, *Mapping the Heavens* (London, British Library, 1995).

WWU Physics/Astronomy Department, 'Native American Sky', Western Washington University, 2022, https://astro101.wwu. edu/indiansky.html/

3. PREDATORS

American Psychiatric Association, *Diagnostic and Statistical Manual of Mental Disorders, Fifth Edition*, 18 May 2013.

Apelblat, M., 'Majority of rural inhabitants in the EU wants stricter protection of bears, lynxes and wolves', *Brussels Times*, 2 Dec 2023.

Bennett, Paige, 'Rewilding Could Help Limit Warming Beyond 1.5 °C, Scientists Say', *EcoWatch*, 28 Mar 2023, https://www. ecowatch.com/global-warming-solutions-rewilding.html/

Berry, Erica, *Wolfish: The stories we tell about fear, ferocity and freedom* (Edinburgh, Canongate Books, 2022).

Beschta, Robert L. and Ripple, William J., Global Trophic Cascades Program, Oregon State University College of Forestry, 'Large Carnivore Trophic Cascades in Western North America', https://trophiccascades.forestry.oregonstate.edu/presentations/

Blair, Ada, 'Fear of the Dark', DarkSky International Night Matters seminar, 19 Oct 2023, YouTube, https://www.youtube.com/watch?v=6JoyIX6H4pQ/

Blumstein, Daniel T., *The Nature of Fear: Survival Lessons from the Wild* (Cambridge, Massachusetts, Harvard University Press, 2020).

Brown, Joel S., et al., 'The Ecology of Fear: Optimal Foraging, Game Theory and Trophic Interactions', *Journal of Mammalogy*, 80:2 (1999).

Clark, William R., 'Is our tendency to experience fear and anxiety genetic?', *Scientific American*, 6 Mar 2000.

Cleveland Clinic, 'Nyctophobia (Fear of the Dark)', 2022, https://my.clevelandclinic.org/health/diseases/22785-nyctophobia-fear-of-the-dark/

Cromie, William J., 'Researchers find a gene for fear', *Harvard Gazette*, 1 Dec 2005.

Darimont, Chris T. et al., 'The unique ecology of human predators', *Science*, 349:6250 (2015).

Dunn, Rob, *The Wild Life of Our Bodies* (HarperCollins, 2011).

Flyn, Cal, 'Landscape of fear: why we need the wolf', *Guardian*, 24 Nov 2020.

Galchen, Rivka, 'The Myth of the Alpha Wolf', *The New Yorker*, 25 Mar 2023.

Giggs, Rebecca, 'Why We're Afraid of Bats', *The Atlantic*, Nov 2020.

Gilroy, William G., 'Early humans on the menu', *Notre Dame News*, 26 Feb 2006.

Gross, Liza, 'How Fear of Humans Can Ripple Through Food Webs and Reshape Landscapes', *Smithsonian Magazine*, 11 Jul 2017.

Grover, Hannah, 'Leader of the Mangas wolf pack killed following concerns of preying on livestock', *New Mexico Political Report*, 18 Apr 2023.

Hoehl, Stefanie et al., 'Itsy Bitsy Spider . . .: Infants React with Increased Arousal to Spiders and Snakes', *Frontiers in Psychology*. 8:1710 (2017).

Italian Ministry of Ecological Transition, Istituto Superiore per la Protezione e la Ricerca Ambientale ISPRA, 'I risultati del Monitoraggio nazionale del lupo', 12 May 2022, https://www.

isprambiente.gov.it/it/attivita/biodiversita/monitoraggio-nazionale-del-lupo/risultati/

Kimeu, Caroline, 'You can see camel carcasses all over: rural Kenyans face tough new battle with predators', *Guardian*, 25 Apr 2023.

Kosinsky, Matthew, 'Au Naturel: How Humans Separated Themselves From Nature – and Why It's Time to Reconsider', *Keap*, 25 Feb 2020, https://keapcandles.com/blogs/keap/au-naturel-how-humans-separated-themselves-from-nature-and-why-it-s-time-to-reconsider/

Large Carnivore Initiative for Europe, 'Assessment of the conservation status of the Wolf (Canis lupus) in Europe', 2 Sep 2022.

Laundré, John W., et al., 'The Landscape of Fear: Ecological Implications of Being Afraid', *Open Ecology Journal*, 3:1-7 (2010).

Maestas, Aislinn, 'Female Mexican Wolf Captured and Paired with Mate in Captivity', US Fish and Wildlife Service press release, 11 Dec 2023.

McGlashan, Elise M., et al., 'Afraid of the dark: Light acutely suppresses activity in the human amygdala', *PLoS One*, 16:6 (2021).

Mowat, Farley, *Never Cry Wolf* (New York, Open Road, 2015).

Robbins, Jim, 'The Fear Factor: How the Peril of Predators Can Transform a Landscape', *Yale Environment 360*, 11 Apr 2017.

Raynor, Jennifer L. et al., 'Wolves make roadways safer, generating large economic returns to predator conservation', *PNAS*, 118:22 (2021).

Robertson, Dani, 'Darkness isn't dangerous to women', Twitter, 23 Oct 2023, https://mobile.x.com/DaniDarkSkies/status/1716515264110473468/

Robinson, Kirk, 'The Psychology of Wolf Fear and Loathing', Rewilding Earth, 28 Jun 2019, https://rewilding.org/the-psychology-of-wolf-fear-and-loathing/

Seton, Ernest Thompson, *Wild Animals I Have Known* (1898, Project Gutenberg Ebook, 2015).

Smith, Chris, 'Asha the roaming Mexican gray wolf captured in New Mexico', WildEarth Guardians press release, 11 Dec 2023.

Wade, Dave, 'The ecology of fear: Elk responses to wolves in Yellowstone are not what we thought', *Western Confluence*, 6 Jan 2014.

4. Myth

Zanette, Liana Y. and Clinchy, Michael, 'Ecology of fear', *Current Biology*, 29:9 (2019).

Bracken, Gerry, 'The "Rolling Sun" Spectacle of Boheh', The Fr. Michael O'Flanagan History & Heritage Centre, 1996, https://www.carrowkeel.com/sites/croaghpatrick/reek3.html/

Brennan, Sinéad, 'Mourning and warning: tracing the banshee in Mayo lore', *Irish Heritage News*, 12 Oct 2023.

Briggs, Katharine, *An Encyclopedia of Fairies: Hobgoblins, Brownies, Bogies and Other Supernatural Creatures* (New York, Pantheon Books, 1976).

Chambers, Michael, Wild Nephin National Park Monuments & Myths brochure, 2022, https://www.nationalparks.ie/app/uploads/2022/09/Monuments_WildNephin.pdf/

Claffey, Patrick, 'A holy mountain: Croagh Patrick in myth, prehistory and history', *Irish Times*, 18 Nov 2016.

Cuimeanach, Fee, 'Older Than Time: The Myth of the Cailleach, The Great Mother', Wee White Hoose, 18 Jan 2021, https://web.archive.org/web/20241210081524/https://weewhitehoose.co.uk/study/the-cailleach/

Edwards, Eric, 'The Banshee', 2 Aug 2014, https://ericwedwards.wordpress.com/2014/08/02/the-banshee/

Farrell, Brendan, 'Co Mayo's Boheh Stone and the "Rolling Sun" phenomenon', *Irish Central*, 21 Aug 2018.

Gallagher, Michael, 'New book claims to unlock mystery of local stones', *Mayo Live*, 8 Sep 2023.

Gillespie, Tom, 'Climbing Croagh Patrick in the dark of night', *Connaught Telegraph*, 27 Jul 2023.

Irish Peatland Conservation Council, 'Blanket Bogs', https://www.ipcc.ie/a-to-z-peatlands/peatland-habitat-types/blanket-bogs/

Horowitz, Anthony, *Myths and Legends* (London, Kingfisher, 2007).

Jones, T. Llew and Jones, Jac, Clarke, Gillian (Transl.), *One Moonlit Night* (UK, Pont Books @Lolfa, 2015).

Kerrigan, Jo, *Old Ways, Old Secrets: Pagan Ireland, Myth, Landscape, Tradition* (Dublin, The O'Brien Press, 2015).

Knight, Jasper, 'Subglacial processes from drumlins in Clew Bay, western Ireland', *Earth Surface Processes and Landforms*, 41:2 (2015).

Kushner, Dale M., 'The Night Sea Journey: Lunar Consciousness and The Hero', *Psychology Today*, 27 Aug 2016.

Lary, Morris H., 'The Banshee: The Wailing Fairy Woman of Ireland', History Cooperative, 7 Oct 2024.

Locke, Tony, *Mayo Folk Tales* (Cheltenham, The History Press, 2014).

Macmillan, Georgia, 'Protecting Our Night Sky Heritage' report, Mayo Dark Skies Community Group, 2018.

Martin, Juliette F., 'Celtic Womanhood and the Banshee', *Unbound*, 27 Aug 2018.

Massey, Eithne, *The Turning of the Year: Lore and Legends of the Irish Seasons* (Dublin, The O'Brien Press, 2021).

Mayo-Ireland, 'Grace O'Malley the Pirate Queen, History in Co. Mayo' https://www.mayo-ireland.ie/en/about-mayo/history/grace-omalley-the-pirate-queen.html/

Muir, Nichole, *The Unseen Realms: A Journey through the Underworld with the Dark Goddesses of Mythology* (independently published, 2023).

Murphy, Anthony, 'Live Irish Myths, Episode #120: Constellations in Irish Mythology', YouTube, https://www.youtube.com/watch?v=oB5Ta0-Kh-M/

Murphy, Anthony and Moore, Richard, *Island of the Setting Sun: In Search of Ireland's Ancient Astronomers* (Dublin, The Liffey Press, 2006).

Narayanan, Priya, *Demons and Demonesses of Hindu Mythology* (New Delhi, Rupa Publications, 2021).

Scuffle, Kate. 'Keening | Celtic Cultural Minute', WDIY Lehigh Valley Public Radio , 8 Apr 2022.

Olcott, William Tyler, *Star Lore: Myths, Legends and Facts* (Mineola, New York, Dover Publications, 2004).

Rainbolt, Dawn, 'Irish Folklore, Myths & Legends: The Hag of Beara', *Wilderness Ireland*, 26 Jul 2017, https://www. wildernessireland.com/blog/hag-beara-irish-myths-legends/

Robinson, H. S. and Wilson, K., *The Encyclopaedia of Myths & Legends of all Nations* (Littlehampton Book Services Ltd, 1967).

Roth, Susan L., *The Story of Light* (Macmillan/McGraw-Hill School Publishing Company, 1990).

Royal Museums Greenwich, 'The extraordinary life of Grace O'Malley', https://www.rmg.co.uk/stories/grace-o-malley-pirate-history-fact-fiction-legend/

Terra Firma Ireland, 'Stories of the Stars', 17 Aug 2020, https://terrafirmaireland.com/stories-of-the-stars/

Trowbridge, Benjamin, 'Meeting Grace O'Malley, Ireland's pirate queen', The National Archives, 16 Jun 2016, https://blog. nationalarchives.gov.uk/meeting-grace-omalley-irelands-pirate-queen/

Mackenzie, Donald A., *Wonder Tales from Scottish Myth and Legend* (Dover Publications, 1997).

Steidle, Anna and Werth, Lioba, 'Freedom from constraints: Darkness and dim illumination promote creativity', *Journal of Environmental Psychology*, vol. 35 (2013).

Weadick, Sharon, 'The Winter Solstice at Newgrange', National Museum of Ireland.

Wilson, Amanda, 'Descent into Darkness with the Cailleach', *Modern Witch*, Medium.com., 7 Nov 2018.

Winterson, Jeanette, 'Why I adore the night', *Guardian*, 31 Oct 2009.

Women's Museum of Ireland, 'Grace O'Malley', https://www. womensmuseumofireland.ie/exhibits/blog-post-title-one-jwrz7/

Wylie, Olivia, 'The History Of The Cailleach Bheara, Queen of Samhain', The Brehon Academy, 1 Oct 2021, https:// brehonacademy.org/the-history-of-the-cailleach-bheara-queen-of-samhain/

5. Early Astronomy

Academy of Sciences of the Republic of Uzbekistan, 'History of development of Uzbek science', https://academy.uz/en/page/ozbekistonda-ilm-fan-taraqqiyoti/

Batchelor, Daud Abdul-Fattah, 'Al-Bīrūnī: Outstanding "Modern" Scientist of the Golden Age of Islamic Civilisation', International Institute of Advanced Islamic Studies, 16 Dec 2015.

Berry, Arthur, *A Short History of Astronomy* (New York, Charles Scribner's Sons, 1899).

Chtatou, Mohamed, 'Reflecting On Islam In The Asian Continent – Analysis', *Eurasia Review*, 12 Aug 2023, https://www.eurasiareview.com/12082023-reflecting-on-islam-in-the-asian-continent-analysis/

Couper, Heather and Henbest, Nigel, *The Story of Astronomy: How the Universe Revealed its Secrets* (New York, Octopus, 2012).

Euronews, 'Images of the Fixed Stars: Ancient astronomy manuscript resurrected by Uzbek heritage initiative', 16 Sep 2021, https://www.euronews.com/culture/2021/09/16/images-of-the-fixed-stars-ancient-astronomy-manuscript-resurrected-by-uzbek-heritage-initi/

Fowler, Michael, 'How the Greeks Used Geometry to Understand the Stars', Galileo and Einstein: Lectures, University of Virginia, CC BY-SA 3.0. https://galileoandeinstein.phys.virginia.edu/lectures/greek_astro.htm/

Hikmah Project, *The Man Who Unlocked The Universe*, YouTube, 19 Feb 2022. https://www.youtube.com/watch?v=vI_7Rj7NLBE/

Hookham, Hilda, 'Ulugh-beg: Star-Gazer in Samarkand', *History Today*, 20:3 (1970).

IAU South West and Central Asian Regional Office of Astronomy for Development, 'Uzbekistan', 2020, http://astrotourism.aras.am/uzbekistan/uzbekistan.php/

Ibbotson, Sophie, *Uzbekistan* (London, Bradt, 2019).

International Astronomical Union, 'The Constellations', https://www.iau.org/public/themes/constellations/

Jazra, Fyza Parviz. Zij-i Sultani (2020 ,(زیج سلطانی)), https://web. stanford.edu/~fparviz/more.html/

Knobel, Edward Ball, *Ulugh Beg's Catalogue of Stars* (Washington D.C., Carnegie Institution of Washington, 1917).

Krisciunas, Kevin, Paksoy, H. B. (Ed.), 'Ulugh Beg's Zij', *Central Asian Monuments* (ISIS Press, 1992).

Li Chih-Ch'ang, Transl. Arthur Waley, *The Travels of an Alchemist: The Journey of the Taoist Ch'ang-Ch'un from China to the Hindukush at the Summons of Chingiz Khan* (London, George Routledge & Sons, 1938).

Library of Congress, 'Astronomical Innovation in the Islamic World', https://www.loc.gov/collections/finding-our-place-in-the-cosmos-with-carl-sagan/articles-and-essays/modeling-the-cosmos/astronomical-innovation-in-the-islamic-world/

Luminet, Jean-Pierre, 'Ulugh Beg, Prince of Stars', ArXiv E-Prints, Apr 2018.

Maidanak Astronomical Observatory, 'About Maidanak', http://www.maidanak.uz/about.php/

Marshall, David Weston, *Ancient Skies: Constellation Mythology of the Greeks* (New York, The Countryman Press, 2018).

Met Museum, 'Unit Four: Science and the Art of the Islamic World', https://www.metmuseum.org/learn/educators/curriculum-resources/art-of-the-islamic-world/unit-four/

Moore, Sir Patrick, *Watchers of the Stars* (London, Michael Joseph Ltd, 1974).

Pennington, R., 'Islam in Uzbekistan', Muslim Voices, http://muslimvoices.org/islam-in-uzbekistan/

Ragep, Dr F. Jamil, *Islamic Astronomy and Copernicus* (Ankara, Turkish Academy of Sciences Publications, 2022).

Silk Roads Programme, 'Caravanserais: cross-roads of commerce and culture along the Silk Roads', Unesco, https://en.unesco.org/silkroad/content/caravanserais-cross-roads-commerce-and-culture-along-silk-roads/

Stirone, Shannon, 'How Islamic scholarship birthed modern astronomy', Astronomy.com, 14 Feb 2017, https://www.astronomy.com/science/how-islamic-scholarship-birthed-modern-astronomy/

REFERENCES

Ulugh Beg, *Zīj-i jadīd-i sulṭānī*, 1487–1488 CE. MS. Greaves 5, Bodleian Library, Oxford University.

UZ Daily, 'Astronomers in Uzbekistan discover new minor planet', 10 Aug 2010.

Walker, Stephen, *Beyond: The Astonishing Story of the First Human to Leave our Planet and Journey Into Space* (London, William Collins, 2021).

Waugh, Daniel C., 'Samarkand', University of Washington, 2005, https://depts.washington.edu/silkroad/cities/uz/samarkand/samark.html/

Wriggins, Sally Hovey, *The Silk Road Journey with Xuanzang* (Cambridge, Massachusetts, Westview Press, 2004).

6. Cosmos

Butterworth, Jon, Scaife, Anna, Nuttall, Laura, and Williams, Sarah, 'Giant Experiments Cosmic Questions' panel talk, Future Circular Collider Study, The Royal Society, YouTube, 8 June 2023, https://www.youtube.com/watch?v=ain50wcB2-8/

Brahmali, Ajahn, 'Buddhist Cosmology: The Unlikely Parallels between the Buddha's Vision & Modern Understandings', The Fourth Messenger: Teachings and Art from the Sangha, 5 Jul 2021, https://www.fourthmessenger.org/authors/ajahn-brahmali/

Center for Astrophysics, 'Dark Energy and Dark Matter', Harvard & Smithsonian, https://www.cfa.harvard.edu/research/topic/dark-energy-and-dark-matter/

Chumikchan, Rinchen Angmo, 'Ladakh short of Astrologers (Onpos)', *Reach Ladakh Bulletin*, 13 Jun 2015, https://www.reachladakh.com/news/religion-spiritual/ladakh-short-of-astrologers-onpos/

Clegg, Brian, *Dark Matter & Dark Energy: The Hidden 95% of the Universe* (London, Icon Books, 2019).

Cliff, Harry, *Space Oddities: The Mysterious Anomalies Challenging Our Understanding of the Universe* (London, Picador, 2024).

Ibbotson, Sophie and Stuart Butler, *Ladakh, Jammu & the Kashmir Valley* (London, Bradt, 2019).

Kelényi, Béla, 'The Myth of the Cosmic Turtle According to the Late Astrological Tradition', *Proceedings of the Ninth Seminar of the IATS, Impressions of Bhutan and Tibetan Art*, vol. 3, 2002.

Marsden, A. J. and Nesbitt, William, 'Myths of Light and Dark', *Psychology Today*, 8 May 2018.

Men-Tsee-Khang Tibetan Medical & Astro Institute, 'Introduction to Tibetan Astro-Science', https://mentseekhang.org/introduction-to-tibetan-astrology/

NASA Science, 'Dark Matter & Dark Energy', https://science.nasa.gov/universe/dark-matter-dark-energy/

Office of Astronomy for Development, 'New Astrostays Model Established At A Buddhist Monastery', 2021, https://astro4dev.org/new-astrostays-established-at-a-buddhist-monastery/

Shen Shián, 'Significance of Clockwise Circumambulation', *Moonpointer: Buddhist Blog of Everyday Dharma*, 10 Nov 2009, https://moonpointer.com/new/2009/11/significance-of-clockwise-circumambulation/

Sims-Williams, Ursula, 'Jai Singh's Observatories', Asian and African studies blog, British Library, 7 Apr 2013, https://blogs.bl.uk/asian-and-african/2013/04/jai-singhs-observatories.html/

Thera, K., Sri Dhammananda Maha, *BuddhaSasana*, 'What Buddhists Believe, Chapter 17 – Divination and Dreams, Astrology and Astronomy', https://www.budsas.org/ebud/whatbudbeliev/312.htm/

Wang, Eva, Transl., *Harmonizing Yin and Yang* (Boston, Massachusetts, Shambhala Publications, 1997).

7. Shadow Work

Arya, Pasang Y., Tibetan Astrology, Tibetanmedicine-edu.org, Dec 2009, https://tibetanmedicine-edu.org/wp-content/uploads/2022/05/tibetan_astrology.pdf

Bassett-Lowe, Briony, 'The History and Development of Meditation', British School of Meditation Blog, 2 Mar 2024,

REFERENCES

https://www.teaching-meditation.co.uk/More/BSOM-Blog/
ArticleID/9/The-History-and-Development-of-Meditation/

Brown Taylor, Barbara, *Learning to Walk in the Dark* (London, Canterbury Press, 2015).

Chia, Mantak, *Darkness Technology: Darkness Techniques for Enlightenment* (Chiang Mai, Universal Tao Publications, 2002).

Clarke, Lee, 'The Buddhist and Taoist influences that underpin the Star Wars universe', *The Conversation*, 6 Dec 2022.

Cleveland Clinic, 'Vestibular System', 19 Jun 2024, https://my.clevelandclinic.org/health/body/vestibular-system/

Geisshuesler, Flavio A., *Tibetan Sky-Gazing Meditation and the Pre-History of Great Perfection Buddhism* (London, Bloomsbury, 2024).

John, Saskia, *Retreat Into Darkness: A Path to Light*, Transl. Gabriele Fröhlich (Bielefeld, tao.de, 2012).

Johnson, Russell P., 'This is the Way: Daoist Themes in Star Wars', The University of Chicago Divinity School, 3 May 2023, https://divinity.uchicago.edu/sightings/articles/way-daoist-themes-star-wars/

Jung, Carl, *Collected Works of C. G. Jung Vol 13: Alchemical Studies* (Princeton, New Jersey, Princeton University Press, 1992).

Mackenzie, Vicki, *Cave in the Snow: A Western Woman's Quest for Enlightenment* (London, Bloomsbury, 1998).

May, Gerald G., *The Dark Night of the Soul: A Psychiatrist Explores the Connection Between Darkness and Spiritual Growth* (New York, HarperCollins, 2004).

Moyers, Bill, interview: 'The Mythology of "Star Wars"' with George Lucas, 18 Jun 1999, https://billmoyers.com/content/mythology-of-star-wars-george-lucas/

Myers, Scott, 'Reflections on Carl Jung (Part 3): Make the Darkness Conscious', *Medium*, Go Into The Story, 12 Sep 2018, https://gointothestory.blcklst.com/reflections-on-carl-jung-part-3-make-the-darkness-conscious-69462e2b5b06/

National Eye Institute, 'How the Eyes Work', 20 Apr 2022 https://www.nei.nih.gov/learn-about-eye-health/healthy-vision/how-eyes-work

Popova, Maria, 'Live the Questions: Rilke on Embracing

Uncertainty and Doubt as a Stabilizing Force', *The Marginalian*, https://www.themarginalian.org/2012/06/01/rilke-on-questions/

Raymo, Chet, *The Soul of the Night: An Astronomical Pilgrimage* (Cambridge, Massachusetts, Cowley Publications, 1992).

Red Pine, Transl., *Lao-tzu's Taoteching* (Copper Canyon Press, 1996).

Sage Blue, 'The Dark Feminine in Daoism: Embracing and Understanding Yin', *Medium*, 11 Mar 2023, https://medium.com/@centinaalexa/the-dark-feminine-in-daoism-embracing-and-understanding-yin-f92c91c9c890/

Salisbury Meditation, 'The history of meditation and how it has developed', https://salisburymeditationandsoundtherapy.co.uk/history-of-meditation/

St John of the Cross, *Dark Night of the Soul*, E. Allison Peers, Transl. (Mineola, New York, Dover Publications, 2003).

Tubbs, Andrew S. et al., 'The Mind After Midnight: Nocturnal Wakefulness, Behavioral Dysregulation, and Psychopathology', *Frontiers in Network Physiology*, 1:830338 (2022).

Wang, Robin R., 'Yinyang (Yin-yang)', Internet Encyclopedia of Philosophy, Loyola Marymount University, https://iep.utm.edu/yinyang/

Westmoquette, Mark, *The Mindful Universe: A journey through the inner and outer cosmos* (London, Leaping Hare Press, 2020).

8. LIFE

Barnes, Christopher and Passmore, Holli-Anne, 'Development and testing of the Night Sky Connectedness Index (NSCI)', *Journal of Environmental Psychology,* 93:102198, Feb 2024.

Burns, A.C. et al., 'Day and night light exposure are associated with psychiatric disorders: an objective light study in >85,000 people', *Nature Mental Health,* 1:853–862, 9 Oct 2023.

Fabian, Samuel T. et al., 'Why flying insects gather at artificial light', *Nature Communications*, 15:689, 30 Jan 2024.

ffrench-Constant, Richard H. et al. 'Light pollution is associated

with earlier tree budburst across the United Kingdom',
Proceedings of the Royal Society B, 283:1833, 29 Jun 2016.

Gaston, Kevin J. et al., 'The ecological impacts of nighttime light
pollution: a mechanistic appraisal', *Biological Reviews*, 88:4, 8
Apr 2013.

Goulson, Dave, *Silent Earth: Averting the Insect Apocalypse* (Dublin,
Penguin Random House, 2021).

Hore, Peter J. and Mouritsen, Henrik, 'How Migrating Birds Use
Quantum Effects to Navigate', *Scientific American*, 1 Apr 2022.

International Astronomical Union Office of Astronomy for
Development. Flagship Project 2: Astronomy for Mental Health,
https://astro4dev.org/themes/theme-2-celebrating-our-
common-humanity-through-astronomy/astronomy-mental-
health/

Jarvis, Brooke, 'The Insect Apocalypse Is Here', The *New York Times
Magazine*, 27 Nov 2018,

Keltner, Dacher, *Awe: The Transformative Power of Everyday Wonder*
(London, Allen Lane, 2023).

Kornreich, Ar, et al., 'Rehabilitation outcomes of bird-building
collision victims in the Northeastern United States', *PLoS One*,
19:8, 7 Aug 2024.

Kraus, Louis J., 'Human and Environmental Effects of Light
Emitting Diode (LED) Community Lighting H-135.927',
American Medical Association Report of the Council on
Science and Public Health, 2016.

Matthews, Karen. 'Hundreds of migrating songbirds crash into
NYC skyscrapers', Associated Press, 16 Sep 2021.

Motta, Mario E., 'We're All Healthier Under a Starry Sky', *AMA
Journal of Ethics*, 26:10, Oct 2024.

Obayashi, Kenji et al., 'Associations between indoor light pollution
and unhealthy outcomes in 2,947 adults: Cross-sectional analysis
in the HEIJO-KYO cohort', *Environmental Research,* 215:2,
Dec 2022.

Rice, Tony, 'Changing sunrise, sunset affects animals as well',
WRAL News, 29 Oct 2013, https://www.wral.com/story/
chaning-sunrise-sunset-affects-animals-as-well/13048961/

Roddick, Charlotte M. et al., 'Effects of near-infrared radiation in ambient lighting on cognitive performance, emotion, and heart rate variability', *Journal of Environmental Psychology*, 100:102484, 2024.

Sample, Ian, 'Why are moths attracted to lights? Science may finally have an answer', *Guardian*, 30 Jan 2024.

Steidle, Anna and Lioba Werth, 'Freedom from constraints: Darkness and dim illumination promote creativity', *Journal of Environmental Psychology*, vol. 35, Sep 2013.

Victor Change Cardiac Research Institute, 'Noise and light pollution could be impacting your heart health', 10 Oct 2023, https://www.victorchang.edu.au/blog/noise-light-pollution-heart-disease/

Xu, Yu-xiang et al., 'Association of light at night with cardiometabolic disease: A systematic review and meta-analysis', *Environmental Pollution*, 342:1, 1 Feb 2024.

9. Love

Bergunker, Victoria, 'Yvytú Porá, un recorrido ancestral en medio de la selva misionera', *El Territorio*, 5 Jan 2020.

Connors, Philip, *Fire Season: Field Notes from a Wilderness Lookout* (London, Macmillan, 2011).

Davis, Nicola, 'Scientists find oldest known evidence of humans in Europe using fires to cook', *Guardian*, 18 May 2023.

Direcçion de Turismo Aristóbulo del Valle, 'Sendero Interpretativo Eco Cultural Comunidad Yvytu Porá', https://adelvalleturismo.com.ar/sendero/

Eaves, Megan, 'Alejandro Sommer: A dark sky mission in Argentina', DarkSky International, 28 Jul 2021, https://darksky.org/news/a-dark-sky-mission-in-argentina/

El Diario de Misiones Primera Edicion, 'Conservación del Cielo Oscuro: la magia de las estrellas, el entorno natural y la influencia guaraní', 2 Sep 2023, https://www.primeraedicion.com.ar/nota/100733821/

REFERENCES

conservacion-del-cielo-oscuro-la-magia-de-las-estrellas-el-entorno-natural-y-la-influencia-guarani/

El Diario de Misiones Primera Edicion, 'Yvytu Porá, Aldea guaraní abierta al turismo, 22 Jul 2018', https://www.primeraedicion.com.ar/nota/100001044/yvytu-pora-aldea-guarani-abierta-al-turismo/

Emerging Technology from the arXivarchive page, 'How Far Can the Human Eye See a Candle Flame?', *MIT Technology Review*, 31 Jul 2015, https://www.technologyreview.com/2015/07/31/72658/how-far-can-the-human-eye-see-a-candle-flame/

Escobar, Patricia, 'Astronomía, arte y conservación | Jóvenes artistas misioneros plasmaron en una gran obra comunitaria la cosmovisión guaraní del cielo en la Reserva Yatei', ArgentinaForestal, 1 Oct 2022, https://www.argentinaforestal.com/2022/10/01/plasmaron-en-una-gran-obra-comunitaria-la-cosmovision-guarani-del-cielo-en-la-reserva-yatei/

Faraday, Michael, *The Chemical History of a Candle* (CreateSpace Independent Publishing Platform, Namaskar Books, 15 Nov 2016).

Ferrer, Aldo, Urquidi, Marjory M. (Transl.), *The Argentine Economy: An Economic History of Argentina*, (Berkeley, University of California Press, 1967).

Iguazú Viajes, 'Enchanted Leap', https://www.iguazuviajes.com/informacion-util/salto-encantado/

Lacerada, Rodrigo, 'Worlding a Mbya-Guaraní heritage: from dissonant heritage to ontological conflicts', *International Journal of Heritage Studies*, 27:3, Jul 2021.

Lutz, Fayne, 'Area History: The Aura of Angel Fire', Angel Fire Chamber of Commerce, https://angelfirechamber.org/area-facts/area-history/

Mannarino, Juan Manuel, 'Juanita, la cacique guaraní que empodera a través de las artesanías y la defensa de la biodiversidad en Misiones', *Infobae*, 30 Oct 2022.

Ministerio de Turismo y Deportes Argentina, 'La Ruta Natural: Salto Encantado Provincial Park', https://larutanatural.gob.ar/en/must-see/25/salto-encantado-provincial-park/

Modelli, Lais, 'A Guaraní community brings native bees back in the shadow of São Paulo', *Mongabay*, 18 May 2023, https://news. mongabay.com/2023/05/a-guarani-community-brings-native-bees-back-in-the-shadow-of-sao-paulo/

Mythosphere, 'Guaraní Mythology', https://www.folklore.earth/culture/guarani/

Planetario de Montevideo, 'The Guaraní Sky', 8 Apr 2020, https://planetariodemontevideo.wordpress.com/2020/04/08/el-cielo-guarani/

Pulso Turistico, 'Cuña Pirú Lodge – Lejos del estrés, cerca del cielo', 10 Oct 2013, http://www.pulsoturistico.com.ar/mas_informacion.asp?id=2758&titulo=Cuna-Piru-Lodge---Lejos-del-estres,-cerca-del-cielo#google_vignette/

Pyne, Stephen J., *Fire: A Brief History* (Seattle, University of Washington Press, 2001).

SamuraiJack, 'Guarani Mythology: Myths, Legends, And Monsters From Paraguay Part 1', HubPages, 28 Aug 2011, https://discover.hubpages.com/education/GuaraniMythology/

Scott, Andrew C., 'When Did Humans Discover Fire? The Answer Depends on What You Mean By "Discover"', *Time*, 2 Jun 2018.

Servin, Blas, Seminar: Conferencia de la Fundación Misionera de Astronomía Aficionada. Astroturismo Misiones, YouTube, https://www.youtube.com/watch?v=K-Iwrd3pouQ/

Servin, Blas, Seminar: Cosmovisión de los Aché y Guaraní. Gramo Ideas, YouTube, https://www.youtube.com/watch?v=u8M2fwBz8M0/

Reed, Richard K., 'Culture Summary: Guaraní', Human Relations Area Files, 1998, https://ehrafworldcultures.yale.edu/document?id=sm04-000/

Sztutman, Renato, 'When Metaphysical Words Blossom: Pierre and Hélène Clastres on Guaraní Thought', *Common Knowledge*, 23:2, 2017.

The Mission (1986) [Film]. Roland Joffé (dir.) Warner Bros., USA

The Sherpa, 'Guaraní Mythology', Lebarty Mythology & Folklore, https://lebarty.bongchong.com/guarani-mythology/

UNEP-WCMC, 'Protected Area Profile for Iberá from the World

Database on Protected Areas', https://www.protectedplanet.net/16890/

Van Gelderen, Ana, 'Cuña Pirú: el lodge misionero con habitaciones en la copa de los árboles diseñado por una familia de arquitectos', *La Nacion*, 28 Nov 2021.

10. HOPE

Adler Planetarium, 'History', https://www.adlerplanetarium.org/explore/about-us/history/

Alvarez, René Luis, 'A Community that Would Not Take "No" for an Answer: Mexican Americans, the Chicago Public Schools, and the Founding of Benito Juarez High School', *Journal of Illinois History*, 17:1, 2014.

BCIT Planetarium, 'History of Planetariums', British Columbia Institute of Technology, https://commons.bcit.ca/planetarium/history-of-planetariums/

CBS Chicago, 'Little Village Retail Strip Is Second Highest Grossing in City', 14 Oct 2015, https://www.cbsnews.com/chicago/news/little-village-retail-strip-is-second-highest-grossing-in-city/

Chicago Metropolitan Agency for Planning, 'Community Data Snapshot – South Lawndale', Chicago Community Area Series report, Jul 2024, https://www.cmap.illinois.gov/

Keating, Ann Durkin, *Chicago Neighborhoods and Suburbs: A Historical Guide* (Chicago, University of Chicago Press, 2008).

King, Henry C., *Geared to the Stars; the evolution of planetariums, orreries, and astronomical clocks* (Toronto, University of Toronto Press, 1978).

Education, Then, Now, Next Almanac, 'Hunger strike for a new high school in Little Village', *Chicago Reporter*, 8 May 2015.

Enlace Chicago, 'Little Village History', https://www.enlacechicago.org/littlevillagehistory/

Little Village Lawndale High School Campus, 'About Little Village Lawndale High School', https://www.lvlhs.org/our_campus.jsp/

Schmidt, John R., 'South Lawndale, aka Little Village', *WBEZ Chicago*, 20 Mar 2013.

Wingard, Monique, 'Chicago By L: The Story of Little Village', *WTTW*, https://www.wttw.com/chicago-by-l/neighborhoods/little-village/